GINO'S

HEALTHY ITALIAN

FOR LESS

Gino D'Acampo

GINO'S

HEALTHY ITALIAN

FOR LESS

HODDER &
STOUGHTON

To my beautiful wife Jessica —
the only woman who can truly
keep me healthy, for less.

CONTENTS

INTRODUCTION

Cooking delicious, satisfying and healthy food on a budget has always been a way of life for Italians. Each generation passes on to the next all the clever tricks and tips we need to feed a family using what is available to us. Food is precious and celebrated, shared and eaten together as a family round the table. And it never goes to waste . . .

We are proud of our cuisine, so whatever we eat tends to be home-made and delicious! Although the younger generations in Italy are indulging more in processed foods nowadays, they are still in a minority compared to other western nations; the majority are continuing to cook in the traditional way, using the wonderful fresh, seasonal ingredients that we're so lucky to have at our fingertips.

Everyone wants to feel well and eat well and, as scientists inform us, the Mediterranean diet is a really good way to achieve both. A 2013 study by researchers from several Spanish universities found that people following a Mediterranean diet had, on average, a 30 per cent lower risk of heart disease and stroke.

The Italian way of eating follows this diet, combining fresh fruit and vegetables with starchy ingredients, a small amount of meat, and oily fish at least twice a week; this creates a diet that is low in cholesterol, low in fat and packed with fibre, vitamins and minerals. And what's more, it always tastes good and will keep everyone full and satisfied throughout the day. Snacking is not part of the Italian way of life, which is another reason why Italians have one of the lowest obesity rates in the world.

The key to the Mediterranean diet lies not just in the produce itself, but also in the fact that the food is home-made, with very little that is processed. This means that you can eat well without having to avoid your favourite foods. I can't resist pizza and pasta, not to mention the odd sweet treat, and I can have all these things – in moderation – because I know what's gone into them and I know I am using the best, freshest ingredients.

Eatwell Plate nutritional guidelines

The Mediterranean diet is similar to the guidelines laid out by the Food Standards Authority in the UK with its Eatwell Plate, which shows the foods needed for a balanced diet and their relative proportions.

Carbohydrates

Approximately one-third of your meals should be starchy carbohydrates, such as bread, pasta, rice or potatoes. If you can, choose wholegrain varieties for extra fibre.

5 a Day

Try to eat at least five portions of different fruits and vegetables each day (see page 19 for more on this).

Protein

Try to eat a little lean protein each day – meat, eggs, beans or pulses and other non-dairy sources, plus at least two portions of fish each week, one of which should be oily, such as mackerel or salmon.

Dairy

Include some milk, cheese and yogurt. These are great sources of protein and calcium but can be high in fat but should be eaten in moderation.

Treat foods

Eat only a small amount of foods that are high in fat and/or sugar every week, such as biscuits, cakes, ice cream and soft drinks.

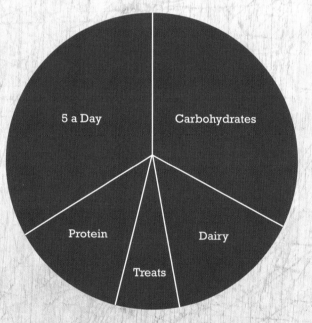

The recipes in this book have been devised with all these guidelines in mind, and each with an upper limit of 650 calories. Of course, some recipes are closer to that count than others, depending on whether they are a main course or a treat, so be sensible when planning your meals – if you are preparing a more calorific meal, make sure that the other two meals of the day are not equally high in calories, fat or salt. And don't snack. Not only is this a really expensive way to eat, but it's also very unhealthy – you won't be able to keep track of what you are eating, which will load you up with empty calories.

Like most Italians, I include oil, butter and cheese in my dishes, but because these are high-fat ingredients, I keep quantities to a minimum. Also, I don't need too much of them because most Italian food uses natural flavourings, particularly herbs, which have barely any calories. I do use salt, too, but again, no more than necessary. If you are on a diet that heavily restricts such ingredients, check the nutrient counts listed on each recipe and make a judgement. Whenever you cook, though, you should taste before you season. It's all about the flavours, so how will you know what it needs if you don't try it first?

In this book I want to prove that it's really easy to eat healthily, but this time I want to show that you can also do it on a budget. Although food prices have soared in recent years and sticking to a budget has become more of a challenge, particularly if we want to eat well, my style of eating is not expensive. All my recipes in this book use everyday ingredients that you can get from your high-street supermarket or local market – you don't need to go to any specialist shops or trawl the internet for weird and expensive ingredients.

The recipes in this book will feed four people for £5, but I've also included recipes to feed friends or larger families – these also work on a budget of £1.25 per head. I've costed them based on the average prices across four major supermarkets in the winter of 2016. Obviously, prices change for certain ingredients according to their season (see Seasonal Calendar, page 10), and other factors, from the state of the economy to the climate, mean we may face further rises in food prices with some foods becoming much more expensive. I've included tips throughout to give you ideas on how to ring the changes according to what's in season or what you have in the cupboards and there are plenty of handy little tricks to get the most delicious results from the recipes.

Eating with the seasons

The majority of fruits and vegetables are seasonal, which means they are grown at specific times of the year in certain countries and their availability affects their market price. If an ingredient is in season, it is therefore abundant and so the price goes down, and if it has been grown locally the costs involved in transporting it from grower to buyer will be lower and are reflected in the price you pay. However, if you are eating something that is out of season in the UK, the price will be higher as it will either have been imported from another country or will have been produced locally but under forced conditions, needing expensive processes such as additional heating. So wherever you can, try to eat seasonally, and you will see the difference in your shopping bills!

Seasonal calendar for locally grown fruit and veg

	SPRING March–May	SUMMER June–Aug	AUTUMN Sept–Nov	WINTER Dec–Feb
FRUIT	Rhubarb	Apples Blueberries Cherries Elderflowers Plums Raspberries Rhubarb Strawberries	Apples Blackberries Pears Plums Strawberries	Apples Pears
VEG	Asparagus Cauliflower Cucumber New potatoes Purple sprouting broccoli Kale Radishes Savoy cabbage Spinach Spring greens Spring onions Watercress	Aubergine Beetroot Broad beans Broccoli Carrots Courgettes Cucumber Fennel Green beans Lettuce New potatoes Peas Rocket Salad onions Spinach Tomatoes Watercress	Beetroot Carrots Celeriac Celery Fennel Field mushrooms Kale Leeks Lettuce Marrow Potatoes Rocket Spinach Squashes Sweetcorn Tomatoes Watercress	Beetroot Cabbage Cauliflower Celeriac Chicory Fennel Jerusalem artichoke Kale Leeks Parsnips Potatoes Red cabbage Swede Turnips

(source: www.lovebritishfood.co.uk/british-food-and-drink/fruit-and-vegetables)

Sensible shopping

Cooking healthily and on a budget isn't complicated and needn't be a chore. In fact, it might even get you really excited about food shopping. Being more aware of what you are buying and cooking from scratch means you can really get in touch with the food you eat, savouring the smells, flavours and rainbow of colours that can fill your plate. And, of course, it is much cheaper than buying ready-made meals.

Even on a budget, it's still worth getting the best-quality foods you can afford, particularly when it comes to ingredients that you need only a little of to get maximum flavour, such as balsamic vinegar and herbs. Shop around for the best prices; try the larger supermarket chains, but also look in street markets for fresh, local produce.

Portion sizes

One of the most sensible approaches to eating a healthy diet on a budget is to think about portion sizes. It's not only good for your weight, but also your wallet. If you keep the portion sizes down, you need to buy less food. It's that simple. In all the recipes in this book I have carefully weighed out the ingredients to meet the calorie counts. If you are not used to looking at your food in this way, it may seem irritating to weigh out ingredients like pasta rather than chuck a handful (or several handfuls) into a saucepan of boiling water, but you'll be amazed at how much you are overeating when you've done it. Pretty soon you'll be able to recognise the amount you need by sight; you'll get used to the smaller portions and you'll find you won't want to eat as much.

If in doubt, go smaller on your portions – there's no point in cooking extra food that just gets wasted, or in feeling unhealthy pressure to clear your plate. If you struggle with portion sizes, one really good trick is to use a smaller plate!

FOOD TYPE	WEIGHT	PORTION SIZE	CALORIES
Pizza	160g	⅓ of a standard dinner plate	395kcal
Cooked rice	150g	A tennis ball	205kcal
Nuts	30g	2 level tbsp	180kcal
Wine	125ml	1 small wine glass	95kcal
Olive oil	11g	1tbsp	100kcal
Cooked pasta	150g	A tennis ball	155kcal
Chocolate (from a bar)	28g	4 small squares from a large bar	146kcal
Cooked lean meat and oil rich fish	80g	A deck of playing cards	170kcal
Cooked white fish	150g	A smartphone	115kcal
Cheese	30g	A small match-box or 3 level tbsp grated	125kcal
Lasagne	290g	A smartphone	415kcal

My storecupboard essentials

In Italy, and particularly in the South, we grow much of our own food to harvest and store – consequently, we use a lot of dried or preserved ingredients in our recipes. Traditionally, harvested crops such as tomatoes, lemons, olives and olive oil, pulses and beans are preserved in oils, dried or pickled, so that we can eat them throughout those months of the year when these are not available as fresh produce. Of course, today's modern processing methods mean that you can eat well all year round, with most of the nutrients of the fresh version being preserved with the ingredient.

I can't ignore my roots, so there are some ingredients I just have to have on standby in the kitchen; these are brilliant back-ups on days when you are pushed for time to cook or haven't been shopping, and they make up the base of much Italian cooking.

These are some of the ingredients I love to have in my cupboards so I can throw together something delicious, healthy and inexpensive without a last-minute trip to the shops. With these in your kitchen there's no excuse for nipping out to buy an expensive processed ready meal!

TIP: Frozen, tinned and dried goods tend to have a long shelf life but always check the use-by dates. When you stock up, make sure you use the older packets or tins first so you don't end up wasting food and throwing stuff away.

Pasta, rice and polenta

Pasta, rice and polenta are fantastic staples and make a filling, quick meal. Although low in fat, these ingredients, particularly pasta, have been demonised by some diet groups because of their high carbohydrate levels. However, health groups are now paying attention to the argument for including carbs as part of a healthy balanced diet and, provided you don't eat huge portions, pasta, rice, bread and other carbs are seen as beneficial. There is no scientific evidence to show that eating carbs means extra calories; it's what you eat them with that causes the problem – such as cream-based sauces – along with the size of the portions.

Pasta

The UK's Eatwell Plate (see page 8) recommends that starchy carbohydrates should make up one-third of the food we eat. Carbs are important for energy and will keep you feeling fuller for longer. Unlike many other sources of carbohydrate, such as bread, potatoes and couscous, pasta has a low glycaemic index (GI), which means it releases sugar into the blood slowly and steadily, avoiding blood sugar spikes. Pasta also contains key minerals and vitamins B1 and B3.

In Italy we have over 600 different types of pasta. We can be quite particular about it because certain sauces are meant only for specific shapes. Now, I'm not suggesting you go crazy and cram your cupboards full of a hundred different varieties, but it's a good idea to keep a supply of dried pasta in a range of shapes and sizes to keep mealtimes interesting!

There is an endless choice of sauces you can make to accompany pasta, most of which, again, make use of storecupboard ingredients such as tinned tomatoes, anchovies and olives. Often you can make sauces using leftovers from other meals. And don't forget – if you have pasta with a tomato sauce packed with veg and topped with a little Parmesan, you are eating from every part of the Eatwell Plate in one meal!

> **TIP:** Pasta cooked until al dente has a lower GI than overcooked, soft pasta, so there's another reason for not cooking pasta too long!

> **TIP:** Cold pasta has a lower GI than hot, so use the leftovers in a salad the next day!

Rice

Rice doesn't make a big appearance in Italian cuisine, except in the classic risotto. For this dish we use a finer type of rice, either Arborio or Carnaroli. Risotto rice contains beneficial starchy carbs for energy and can create a dish that seems rich without being calorifically so, because when cooked it has a creamy texture and is very filling.

Polenta

Although this is traditionally a peasant food, polenta has now worked its way into the everyday diet of all Italians. It is cheap to buy and really versatile – as well as really quick to cook. We use it as a substitute for pasta, rice or potatoes, as a similar source of carbohydrates. You can cook it to a consistency like mashed potato, leave it to set and serve it in slices, or use it raw instead of breadcrumbs to add a crunchy texture to chicken, meat or fish.

Pulses and beans

Pulses and beans are a real staple of the Italian diet; inexpensive but immensely satisfying, they make an excellent protein substitute for more expensive meat, or can be used to pad out a stew or soup to reduce the amount of meat needed, thereby lowering costs. Pulses and beans are low GI, low in fat and high in fibre, so you need only a small amount to make you feel full. They are nutritional powerhouses, containing a range of vitamins and minerals including iron, to keep blood healthy and to prevent anaemia, magnesium for building strong bones, and phosphorus, copper and zinc.
I tend to use a lot of chickpeas, cannellini beans, borlotti beans and lentils and they are just as nutritious whether you buy them dried or tinned. Obviously, tinned are much easier and more useful if you are pressed for time, as you just open the tin and drain them, with no overnight soaking needed. However, if you do buy tinned, make sure you buy them without added salt.

Tinned tomatoes

Generally I'd say no to tinned veg – why would you do it? Just use fresh. The exception is tomatoes – tins of whole or chopped tomatoes or cartons of passata (sieved tomatoes) are fantastic back-ups that you should always have in your cupboard. They are excellent all-rounders – good for sauces, soups, stews or casseroles. Tomatoes contribute to our 5 a day, are low in fat and calories, provide fibre and are a good source of vitamin C and lycopene, an antioxidant which may reduce risk of heart disease and several types of cancer. Although these health benefits belong to all tomatoes, you might be surprised to know that cooked and tinned tomatoes have a more concentrated source of lycopene than fresh!

TIP: My other exception to the rule on preserved vegetables would be frozen veg. It's always good to have a bag of peas in the freezer, for example, as they are frozen immediately after picking and have a higher nutritional value than the fresh ingredient. They are also much cheaper than fresh peas, even when they are in season.

Olives

These inexpensive little fruits make great snacks, but are also fantastic on pizzas, in pasta sauces, salads and also in stews. Olives are a good source of monounsaturated fats and contain vitamin E and polyphenols. They are high in salt, though, so don't immediately add extra seasoning when cooking with them – taste the dish first!

Anchovies and capers

A must-have in any store cupboard. You can buy them in tins or jars, preserved in oil or brine, and they have a long shelf life. A jar is not expensive and because they have a strong, salty flavour you don't need many to get the full impact! Again, excellent on pizzas, in pasta sauces, salads and stews.

Dried mushrooms

The Italians are great fans of mushrooms – particularly wild ones – and the porcini is one of the kings of the mushroom world. You can get little bags of these dried mushrooms in most supermarkets. They are not cheap, but they have a powerful, earthy flavour once rehydrated, so you don't need many of them in a dish. They are worth the expense and make a fantastic risotto to fill you up on a cold night (see Autumn-inspired Risotto with Mushrooms and Fresh Thyme, page 78).

Onions and garlic

Italian food wouldn't taste the same without onions and garlic – we use one or the other in pretty much every savoury dish! They are also really good for you; as well as contributing to your 5 a day, they are low in calories, a great source of fibre and have anti-bacterial and anti-inflammatory properties. The allicin compound in garlic is thought to reduce the risk of heart attacks, high blood pressure and certain cancers, and regularly eating onions may also help to lower blood sugars.

Herbs and spices

These are great for adding all-important flavour and often mean you can reduce the amount of salt you add to a dish. I prefer to use fresh herbs, as they have a better flavour. Don't waste money buying packets of cut herbs; if you have a sunny windowsill, buy the growing pots you find in the supermarkets, or sow a few seeds of your own. They will last much longer and work out much cheaper. I grow a selection of herbs in a large pot by my back door – it's so easy to nip out and snip a few as I need them. Good herbs to have on standby are: basil, oregano, parsley, rosemary, chives, sage and mint.

I am also a great fan of chillies, whether fresh or dried, to add a little heat to whatever I'm cooking. I like to have a jar of chilli flakes in the cupboard at all times; if you buy a packet of fresh chillies, you can always freeze any you are not using straight away for another time.

Other great flavourings to have to hand are stock cubes in all flavours (meat, chicken, fish, veg) and lemons. Yes, the sharp juice of a humble lemon also means you can cut back on salt. Lemons are also rich in antioxidant vitamin C and limonoid compounds that may help to fight cancer.

TIP: If you do buy cut herbs, trim a little off the stems of leafy herbs and put them in some water, as you would flowers, then cover them loosely with a plastic bag, put them in the fridge and they should stay fresh for at least a week. Woody herbs like thyme and rosemary are better lightly wrapped in damp kitchen paper and layered in open plastic bags.

Oils and vinegars

Olive oil

The more you pay, the better the taste – there really is no other way round it. The more flavourful (read expensive!) it is, however, the less you will need.

Extra virgin olive oil, made from the first pressing of the olives, is the most expensive type and has the strongest flavour; virgin olive oil is a cheaper version, made from a blend of virgin and refined olive oils, and as such has less flavour but is better for cooking, being more stable at high temperatures than extra virgin olive oil.

All olive oils are high in fat, so use them sparingly, but it is a heart-healthy fat. Olive oil is also a rich source of vitamin E and polyphenols, which are antioxidants.

Italians don't really use dressings for salads – we are more likely to simply drizzle some olive oil or balsamic vinegar over salad leaves and vegetables.

Balsamic vinegar

This is another ingredient that is not cheap, but a little goes a long way as the flavour is so rich and intense. The longer balsamic has aged, the better it is – and the more expensive! However, it is worth spending a bit more to get the full impact of its flavour; it keeps really well in a cool, dark cupboard. For the real thing, look for the words *Aceto Balsamico Tradizionale di Modena*, which means it has been produced using traditional methods.

Fresh ingredients

Although I do love a dish made with storecupboard staples, most of the recipes in this book will use some kind of fresh ingredient, all of which are easy to source.

The following form the backbone of most of my recipes, and all are easily available in the shops.

Meat, poultry and fish

You only need these in small amounts. Italians eat less red meat than many other European countries, but more seafood – much of which is oily fish such as sardines, pilchards, anchovies and tuna. These are all rich in Omega 3 fats which are important for a healthy heart, and we are advised to eat at least two portions of fish a week.

Meat and poultry are mostly eaten as main courses, and often feature in stews, where they can be bulked out with cheaper ingredients. When you are on a budget, this is a great way to make meat stretch further for the family. Cooking meat or chicken long and slow in stews means you can really get the full flavours of them and the cheaper cuts are perfect for this style of cooking, such as in Roasted Chicken Legs with Thyme and Chickpeas (see page 120) or Mutton Casserole with Red Wine and Root Vegetables (see page 53). Meat and fish are expensive, though, so why not try to have at least one day a week meat-free? I've included a whole chapter of delicious recipes that don't include either meat or fish, such as Spicy Baked Aubergines with Parmesan Cheese (see page 143).

Egg

In Italy we eat more eggs than many other European nations. They are so good for you and really inexpensive. Eggs are an excellent source of protein, so they are great for breakfast – setting you up for the day and thereby helping to avoid any temptation to snack – or for a hearty lunch. I love cooking omelettes and frittatas – they're the ultimate speedy but satisfying meal and a good way to use up any leftovers in the fridge, which can make varying, interesting fillings.

Cheese

We Italians do like our cheese, but we tend to use small amounts of it, which keeps the calorie count per meal low.

> **TIP:** When buying cheese, a tip that works for your wallet and your waistline is to remember that the stronger the flavour, the less you need to use – choose a more mature cheese for maximum impact.

Parmesan (Parmigiano Reggiano), or the slightly cheaper Grana Padano, will be offered alongside most pasta dishes (except those containing seafood – a big NO!) as well as making an appearance in soups and risottos or being shaved over salads and veg. Parmesan is fairly high in fat and calories, so should be used sparingly. Grana Padano is a less fattening alternative, but both are lower in fat than some popular British cheeses, such as Cheddar; they are also higher in calcium.

Mascarpone adds a wonderful creaminess to sauces and desserts but is high in fat, so in this book I've often recommended using the lower-fat version to keep the calories down.

Mozzarella is the classic favourite for salads and pizzas and again is a higher-fat cheese. You can, however, get reduced-fat versions which are fine for cooking with.

Clever planning

Cutting costs on buying food starts with shopping. Italians tend to shop every day in their local markets or shops – it's as much a sociable thing as to make sure they get the freshest ingredients. However, for the younger generation this isn't as easy as it used to be in their parents' day; with the majority of women working, this is another role that is now shared. Working hours in Italy are not like English ones; you can't pop out in your lunch break to get food for dinner, as the shops shut for a couple of hours so that everyone can go home to eat and spend time with friends and family. And the working day ends later, with a small meal after a big lunch, so a little more planning is needed!

Increasingly, even Italians are having to forfeit the daily shop and get used to keeping a well-stocked kitchen. This doesn't mean you can't eat really healthily, though. A decent storecupboard can provide the base for a number of meals that can be added to with some fresh ingredients that you can keep in the fridge for a few days – or with what you have stored in the freezer.

A little time spent planning ahead and making sure you have all the ingredients in the house to enable you to whip up a family dinner will save you time later when you're in a rush – and you'll save money, too, by not resorting to the easy option of buying ready-made meals. You could go all Italian mamma and spend one evening or one weekend afternoon batch-cooking recipes – perhaps pasta sauces, soups, casseroles or even pizza bases – that you can portion up and put in the freezer ready to pull out when you need them. If time is really short, you could simply cook double the quantity of the recipe and freeze half – recipes like Chilli Con Carne with Fresh Rosemary (see page 186) and Pasta in a Delicious Meat Sauce (see page 36) are great for this – or make the Spicy Ratatouille from page 157 so that part of the dish is prepared ahead.

Don't ignore your leftovers, either – pasta or risotto can make a great lunch the next day, polenta can be fried up as a side dish and frittata are delicious cold in a packed lunch. Think before you throw food away – there is always something you can do with it to make another meal. Old bits of bread, for example, can be whizzed up to make breadcrumbs to coat chicken or fish, as in my Baked Cod with Crispy Parsley Breadcrumbs (see page 166).

Make a list before you go shopping – see what you already have in your kitchen to make sure you don't buy more of the same thing. Have a look at the dates on packets, too; it might be better to use up tins of tomatoes or bags of pasta or rice before you go and buy more of the same.

When it comes to fresh ingredients, buy only what you need and what you think you will use – you don't want to waste anything by chucking it away because you didn't get round to eating it.

Using your freezer

Of course, making good use of fresh ingredients is another good reason for making friends with your freezer – if you know you won't get to use an ingredient immediately after buying it, freeze it as soon as you get home, so you are preserving it at its freshest. It's also worth keeping an eye out for supermarket offers such as 'buy one get one free', or reduced items that are not at their sell-by date, as these can be frozen for another day. Have a look at prices per weight, too; it can be cheaper to buy a larger quantity of meat or chicken, divide it up and freeze it in smaller portions. It is also usually cheaper to buy a whole side of salmon and slice it into portions yourself than to buy the ready-filleted portions. I've suggested using stock cubes throughout this book, and, given that it's cheaper to buy a whole chicken and to portion it up yourself than to buy thighs, breasts and drumsticks separately, you'll find that doing this will leave you with a beautiful chicken carcass for boiling into stock and using in soups like my Creamy Chicken Soup with Basil Pesto (see page 60), or in casseroles. Or you could do this by using the carcass after a roast.

If you are freezing food, a little housekeeping will help:

1. Keep the freezer at a constant temperature of -18°C for optimum storage.

2. If you are freezing cooked food, cool it to room temperature as quickly as possible first – ideally within 2 hours.

3. Always use freezerproof packaging to protect foods and prevent 'freezer burn' – make sure food is properly wrapped in foil, cling film or in its original packaging, or stored in freezerproof, sealable containers.

4. Never freeze anything that has already been frozen and defrosted.

5. Freeze foods in portions and always label the containers with the contents and the date.

6. Home-made food will keep for 2 months in the freezer, raw beef and lamb for 6 months, veal, pork and poultry for 4 months, and fish and seafood for 6 months.

Foods that can't be frozen

The formation of ice crystals during the freezing process can affect the cell membranes of certain foods and so damage their texture or flavour, which means certain ingredients are not suitable for freezing.

These include:

• Vegetables with a high water content – lettuce, cucumber, radishes, mushrooms.

• Ingredients with a higher fat content – egg-based sauces, yogurt, cream and low-fat soft cheese.

5 a day

TIP:
Potatoes do not count as part of your 5 a day, as they mostly contain starch.

We've all heard about 5 a day. With the Italian diet this is easily achieved, as so many of our meals include fresh fruit and vegetables.

These foods play an important part in a healthy diet and scientists across the world have concluded that there are significant health benefits to be gained by eating at least five portions of 80g of fruit and veg each day, including a lowered risk of heart disease, stroke and some cancers. You can take your pick of fruit and vegetables available all year round – all are good sources of vitamins and minerals, including folate, vitamin C and potassium, although quantities vary depending on the fruit or vegetable. They are also an excellent source of dietary fibre, which helps maintain a healthy gut and prevents constipation, and a diet high in fibre can also reduce the risk of bowel cancer.

Most fruit and veg are low in fat and calories, too, which makes them a healthy snack choice – although be warned that dried fruits are higher in calories and sugar than fresh, so should be eaten in smaller quantities.

What is one portion towards your 5 a day?

A single portion should weigh about 80g, which is roughly equivalent to:

1 small apple, orange, banana or pear

1 large slice of melon or pineapple

2 plums, kiwi fruit or satsumas

30g dried fruit

3 tablespoons of cooked vegetables, such as carrots or peas

2 broccoli spears

4 tablespoons of cooked kale

7 cherry tomatoes

3 heaped tablespoons of tinned or cooked cannellini, kidney, borlotti beans or chickpeas

150ml fruit juice (including from concentrate)

Note that this only counts as one portion no matter how much you drink in a day.

For children, a portion is as much as they can hold in their hand.

PASTA

The ultimate healthy fast food. Say goodbye to stodgy sauces that fill your plate and leave you feeling weighed down – these are fresh, flavourful and inspired ideas for using this staple Italian ingredient. From classic meat ragùs and tomato sauces to mouth-watering vegetable or seafood combinations, there are recipes for all the family that are easy to prepare, delicious and good for you.

CLASSIC ROMAN PASTA WITH EGGS, PANCETTA AND PECORINO ROMANO

I bet everyone has eaten this popular Roman dish at some time or another; well, forget all the versions you've eaten before and try this – one of my favourite recipes ever. This is a healthier version of the classic: the egg coats the strands of pasta and adds a sumptuous creaminess . . . which means you don't need to add fattening cream or mascarpone. In fact, I'd say never ever add cream anyway – it would destroy the flavours of this subtle dish.

SERVES 4

2 tablespoons olive oil
20g salted butter
100g diced pancetta
2 eggs
4 tablespoons freshly grated
  Pecorino Romano cheese
4 tablespoons fresh
  flat-leaf parsley, finely
  chopped
400g spaghetti
Salt and freshly ground black
  pepper

1. Place a medium frying pan over a medium heat, add the oil and butter and fry the pancetta for 8 minutes until golden and crispy. Stir occasionally with a wooden spoon and set aside.

2. Whisk the eggs in a medium bowl with half the Pecorino Romano cheese. Stir in the parsley and plenty of black pepper; set aside.

3. Cook the spaghetti in a large saucepan of salted boiling water until al dente. To get the perfect al dente bite, cook the pasta for 1 minute less than instructed on the packet.

4. Meanwhile, place the frying pan with the pancetta back over a medium heat for 2 minutes to heat through.

5. Once the pasta is cooked, drain well and tip back in the same saucepan it was cooked in, off the heat. Pour over the egg mixture and the hot pancetta. Mix all together for 30 seconds. (The heat from the pasta and hot pancetta will be sufficient to cook the eggs enough to get a creamy and moist texture.)

6. Season with salt and pepper and serve immediately with the remaining cheese sprinkled on top.

GINO'S TIP: Serve immediately for the best consistency. If the sauce looks a little dry, add a little pasta cooking water to loosen it.

Per serving	Kcal	Fat	Saturates	Carbs	Sugars	Fibre	Protein	Salt
	642	27g	12g	75g	3g	4g	24g	1.34g

PASTA WITH CHERRY TOMATO SAUCE, PANCETTA AND PECORINO ROMANO

This is perfect for a quick and easy supper at the end of a busy day. Tinned cherry tomatoes are packed with flavour and nutrients, so they are brilliant – essential, even – to have on hand in the cupboard, as well being an inexpensive option when these little fresh juicy treats are out of season.

SERVES 4

3 tablespoons olive oil
1 large red onion, peeled and thinly sliced
½ teaspoon dried chilli flakes
110g diced pancetta
2 x 400g tins of cherry tomatoes
400g fettuccine
3 tablespoons fresh flat-leaf parsley, chopped
60g freshly grated Pecorino Romano cheese
Salt

1. Place a large frying pan over a medium heat, add the oil and fry the onion for 5 minutes, stirring occasionally with a wooden spoon. Add the chilli flakes and the pancetta and continue to cook for a further 8 minutes. Stir occasionally

2. Pour in the cherry tomatoes, stir well and simmer gently for 10 minutes with the lid off, stirring every couple of minutes. Season with salt, remove from the heat and set aside.

3. Cook the pasta in a large saucepan of salted boiling water until al dente. To get the perfect al dente bite, cook the pasta for 1 minute less than instructed on the packet. Once the pasta is cooked, drain and tip back into the same pan it was cooked in.

4. Pour over the cherry tomato sauce with the parsley and stir all together over a medium heat for 30 seconds to allow the flavours to combine fully.

5. Sprinkle the grated Pecorino Romano cheese over the top and serve immediately.

GINO'S TIP: Make sure you toss your perfectly cooked pasta with the sauce to really coat the strands evenly – you want to get the wonderful flavours in every mouthful.

Per serving	Kcal	Fat	Saturates	Carbs	Sugars	Fibre	Protein	Salt
	651	20g	6g	92g	13g	9g	22g	0.83g

PASTA SHELLS WITH SMOKED SALMON, COURGETTE AND YELLOW PEPPERS

This is a fabulously healthy pasta dish, low in saturated fats, sugar and salt – and it looks wonderful, too, with its rainbow of colourful veg and the luscious pink of the smoked salmon pieces. If you're not a big fish eater, like my wife, give this a go; you'll find the smoked salmon flavour is deliciously subtle. For a special dinner with friends, serve this with some chilled Pinot Grigio. *Salute!*

SERVES 4

1 large courgette
4 tablespoons olive oil
1 large red onion, peeled
    and thinly sliced
2 yellow peppers, deseeded
    and thinly sliced
100g smoked salmon,
    roughly chopped
500g conchiglie rigate
Grated zest of 1 unwaxed
    lemon
2 tablespoons chives, finely
    chopped
Salt and freshly ground black
    pepper

1. Coarsely grate the courgette and put into the middle of a clean tea towel. Squeeze over a sink to allow all the water from the courgette to run out.

2. Place a large frying pan over a medium heat, pour in the oil and fry the courgette for 4 minutes, stirring occasionally with a wooden spoon. Add the onion and peppers and continue to cook for a further 5 minutes. Stir occasionally.

3. Add the smoked salmon and continue to cook for 3 minutes, stirring as before. Season with salt and pepper and set aside.

4. Cook the pasta in a large saucepan of salted boiling water until al dente. To get the perfect al dente bite, cook the pasta for 1 minute less than instructed on the packet. Once the pasta is cooked, drain and tip back into the same pan it was cooked in.

5. Place the pan over a medium heat and pour over the smoked salmon mixture, along with the lemon zest and chives. Stir all together for 30 seconds allowing the flavours to combine fully. Serve immediately.

GINO'S TIP: The smoked salmon is the most expensive ingredient in this dish, but to cut costs you can use trimmings rather than slices. They're about half the price, but taste just as good.

Per serving	Kcal	Fat	Saturates	Carbs	Sugars	Fibre	Protein	Salt
	651	16g	2g	99g	10g	10g	24g	0.5g

FUSILLI IN A SIMPLE TOMATO SAUCE WITH FRESH BASIL

Sometimes, less is just more. This couldn't be easier, using a handful of ingredients that most people have in their kitchen to produce a healthy, flavoursome dish in minutes. Tinned tomatoes are not only an inexpensive ingredient but are also essential here because fresh tomatoes will make the sauce watery. Go light or go heavy on the Parmesan – it's your choice – but with good-quality tomatoes and fresh basil there are plenty of flavours going on here.

SERVES 4

4 tablespoons extra virgin olive oil
1 large red onion, peeled and finely chopped
2 x 400g tins of chopped tomatoes
10 basil leaves
400g fusilli
4 tablespoons freshly grated Parmesan cheese
Salt and freshly ground black pepper

1. Place a medium saucepan over a medium heat, add the oil and fry the onions in the oil for 6 minutes, stirring occasionally with a wooden spoon.

2. Pour in the tomatoes and basil, season with salt and pepper and cook over a low heat for 20 minutes with the lid off. Stir every 5 minutes.

3. Cook the fusilli in a large saucepan of salted boiling water until al dente. To get the perfect al dente bite, cook the pasta for 1 minute less than instructed on the packet. Once the pasta is cooked, drain and tip back into the same pan it was cooked in.

4. Pour over the tomato and basil sauce and stir all together for 30 seconds to allow the flavours to combine fully.

5. Serve hot with a little Parmesan cheese sprinkled on top.

Per serving	Kcal	Fat	Saturates	Carbs	Sugars	Fibre	Protein	Salt
	562	13g	2g	90g	13g	8g	16g	0.04g

LINGUINE IN A SPICY TUNA SAUCE WITH OLIVES AND GARLIC

The combination of tuna and tomatoes is always a winner. This sauce is really healthy and using tuna in oil rather than brine lowers the salt content without losing out on flavour. Don't be tempted to serve this pasta dish with any grated cheese on top; it's a real no-no for an Italian and you will ruin the freshness of the sauce.

SERVES 4

4 tablespoons extra virgin olive oil
2 garlic cloves, peeled and thinly sliced
80g pitted Kalamata olives in oil or brine, drained and cut in half
1 teaspoon dried chilli flakes
1 x 400g tin of chopped tomatoes
2 x 160g tins of tuna in oil, drained
2 tablespoons fresh flat-leaf parsley, finely chopped
400g linguine
Salt

1. Put the oil and garlic into a medium frying pan and place over a medium heat. Add the olives and chilli flakes and fry for 3 minutes, stirring occasionally with a wooden spoon.

2. Pour in the chopped tomatoes and continue to cook for a further 8 minutes. Stir occasionally. Scatter the tuna and parsley over the tomato sauce, season with a little salt and stir all together. Remove from the heat and set aside.

3. Cook the pasta in a large saucepan of salted boiling water until al dente (see tip). Once the pasta is cooked, drain and tip back into the same pan it was cooked in.

4. Pour over the tuna sauce, return to a low heat and stir all together for 30 seconds to allow the flavours to combine. Serve hot.

Per serving	Kcal 641	Fat 19g	Saturates 3g	Carbs 84g	Sugars 6g	Fibre 8g	Protein 30g	Salt 1.27g

LINGUINE WITH ANCHOVIES, CHILLI AND GARLIC

In Italy this would traditionally have been served as an inexpensive dish to feed a crowd. It's still a great standby recipe, using ingredients that can mostly be found in storecupboards but which together create something that has great flavours and textures. The gentle kick from the chilli and crunch from freshly toasted breadcrumbs really makes my mouth water! All it needs as an accompaniment is a crisp green salad and a chilled bottle of Vermentino wine.

SERVES 4

3 tablespoons olive oil
3 garlic cloves, peeled and
   cut in half
1 teaspoon dried chilli flakes
4 anchovy fillets in oil,
   drained and chopped
80g fresh white breadcrumbs
500g linguine
3 tablespoons fresh flat-leaf
parsley, chopped
Salt

1. Place a medium frying pan over a low heat, pour in the olive oil and gently fry the garlic until golden all over. Remove the garlic and add the chilli flakes and anchovies to the pan. Cook for about 3 minutes or until the anchovies are melted into the oil, stirring with a wooden spoon. Set aside.

2. Place a clean frying pan over a medium heat and toast the breadcrumbs until crispy and golden brown. Set aside.

3. Cook the linguine in a large saucepan of salted boiling water until al dente. To get the perfect al dente bite, cook the pasta for 1 minute less than instructed on the packet. Once the linguine is cooked, drain and tip back into the same pan it was cooked in.

4. Return the pan of linguine to a low heat and pour over the anchovy oil, chopped parsley and breadcrumbs. Stir it all together for 30 seconds to allow the flavours to combine fully.

5. Serve immediately.

GINO'S TIP: Don't waste the ends of fresh bread loaves. If a loaf is beginning to turn stale, blitz it into crumbs, tip the crumbs into a freezer bag and freeze for use in recipes like this.

Per serving	Kcal	Fat	Saturates	Carbs	Sugars	Fibre	Protein	Salt
	640	11g	2g	110g	4g	8g	20g	0.72g

RIGATONI WITH OLIVES, CHOPPED TOMATOES AND OREGANO

Olives, tomatoes and oregano are classic tastes of the Mediterranean, so close your eyes and let this pasta sauce transport you to Italy! Make sure all the ingredients are the best quality you can afford to make this this inexpensive yet satisfying dish really special.

SERVES 4

3 tablespoons extra virgin olive oil
3 garlic cloves, peeled and thinly sliced
2 x 400g tins of chopped tomatoes
12 pitted black olives in brine, drained and cut in half
2 teaspoons dried oregano
500g rigatoni
Salt and freshly ground black pepper

1. Place a large frying pan over a medium heat, add the oil and fry the garlic for 1 minute. Stir with a wooden spoon.

2. Pour in the chopped tomatoes with the olives and oregano. Stir and gently simmer for 15 minutes with the lid off, stirring every couple of minutes. Season with salt and pepper, remove from the heat and set aside.

3. Cook the pasta in a large saucepan of salted boiling water until al dente. To get the perfect al dente bite, cook the pasta for 1 minute less than instructed on the packet. Once the pasta is cooked, drain and tip back into the same pan it was cooked in.

4. Place the pan of pasta back over a low heat, pour over the pizzaiola sauce and stir it all together for 30 seconds.

5. Serve immediately, preferably with a bottle of Cannonau red wine. *Buon appetito!*

GINO'S TIP: Letting the pasta and sauce sit for 30 seconds before serving allows the flavours to really combine.

Per serving	Kcal	Fat	Saturates	Carbs	Sugars	Fibre	Protein	Salt
	584	11g	2g	98g	10g	9g	18g	0.3g

FILLED PASTA WITH RICOTTA, SPINACH AND BÉCHAMEL SAUCE

My grandfather, Giovanni, created this for my mother about 40 years ago and today we still use the same recipe. It's definitely one to try; it's easy, not expensive to put together and has a real wow factor when you present this to guests. I've used Grana Padano here as it is a less calorific cheese than Parmesan and cheaper to buy, though equally delicious. If you prefer, you can replace it with a good mature Cheddar cheese.

SERVES 6

500g passata (sieved tomatoes)
16 basil leaves
18 cannelloni tubes
30g freshly grated Grana Padano cheese

For the filling
500g ricotta cheese
150g frozen spinach, defrosted and squeezed to remove any excess water, roughly chopped
120g rocket leaves, roughly chopped
¼ teaspoon freshly grated nutmeg
60g freshly grated Grana Padano cheese
Salt and freshly ground black pepper

For the béchamel sauce
70g salted butter
70g plain flour
700ml semi-skimmed milk, cold
¼ freshly grated nutmeg

1. To prepare the filling, put all the ingredients into a large bowl, season with salt and pepper and with the help of a fork, mix all together. Let it rest in a fridge for 20 minutes.

2. To make the béchamel sauce, melt the butter in a medium saucepan over a medium heat. Stir in the flour with a wooden spoon and cook for 1 minute until it becomes a light brown colour. Gradually whisk in the cold milk, reduce the heat and cook for 10 minutes, whisking constantly. Once thickened, stir in the nutmeg. Season with salt and pepper and set aside to cool slightly.

3. Pour the passata into a large bowl, add the basil leaves and season with salt and pepper. Mix everything together well and set aside.

4. Preheat the oven to 190°C/gas mark 5. Meanwhile, stuff each cannelloni tube with about 1½ tablespoons of filling until they are all filled.

5. Find a rectangular baking dish measuring about 22 x 30cm and pour in a third of the béchamel sauce. Spread evenly over the base. Place half of the cannelloni on top of the béchamel sauce with the seams facing down. Spoon over half the passata and half the remaining béchamel sauce. Build up the second layer of cannelloni, followed by the remaining passata and finally the remaining béchamel sauce.

6. Finish by sprinkling over the grated Grana Padano and a little black pepper, then bake in the middle of the oven for 55 minutes.

GINO'S TIP: When the cannelloni is cooked through, leave it to rest for 5 minutes out of the oven – it will be easier to cut and serve because the layers will hold together better.

Per serving	Kcal	Fat	Saturates	Carbs	Sugars	Fibre	Protein	Salt
	550	26g	16g	49g	12g	4g	26g	0.8g

PASTA IN A DELICIOUS MEAT SAUCE

The ultimate comfort food. I love to make this with a mixture of beef and pork because I think the combination of meats gives the sauce a mellower, meatier flavour. To get a melt-in-the-mouth texture, let this cook for a minimum of 2 hours – longer if you have the time.

SERVES 6

2 tablespoons olive oil
1 onion, peeled and finely chopped
1 large carrot, peeled and finely grated
2 celery sticks
350g beef mince
350g pork mince
1 x 690g bottle of passata (sieved tomatoes)
2 tablespoons tomato purée
200ml hot chicken stock
500g fresh tagliatelle
60g freshly grated Parmesan cheese, to serve
Salt and freshly ground black pepper

1. Heat the olive oil in a large saucepan and cook the onion, carrot and celery for 8 minutes over a medium heat. Stir occasionally with a wooden spoon.

2. Add the minced meats and cook for 5 minutes until coloured all over, stirring continuously with a wooden spoon to break up the meat. Season with salt and pepper.

3. Pour in the passata, tomato purée and stock, reduce the heat and cook for 2 hours with the lid off. Stir the sauce every 20 minutes or so with a wooden spoon. Remove from the heat, taste and season with salt and pepper and set aside.

4. Cook the tagliatelle in a large saucepan of salted boiling water until al dente. To get the perfect al dente bite, cook the pasta for 1 minute less than instructed on the packet. Drain and tip back into the same saucepan it was cooked in.

5. Place the saucepan back over a low heat, pour over the ragù sauce and gently stir all together for 30 seconds to allow the flavours to combine fully.

6. Serve with a little Parmesan cheese sprinkled on top.

GINO'S TIP: This is a great sauce to cook in a large batch, bubbling on the stove or in a slow cooker. Freeze the sauce in portions for another day – you'll find that the flavour has often improved when you come to defrost it!

Per serving	Kcal	Fat	Saturates	Carbs	Sugars	Fibre	Protein	Salt
	568	21g	7g	55g	9g	7g	36g	0.42g

PENNE AND A CLASSIC ITALIAN SAUCE WITH RED CHILLIES, GARLIC AND CHOPPED TOMATOES

With such a great combination of flavours, I promise you won't miss the meat! This is the kind of vegetarian dish I can get excited about. The chilli and garlic are heart-healthy ingredients that get the taste buds going without being overpowering. Chuck it all in a pan at the end of a busy day for a really comforting bowl.

SERVES 4

4 tablespoons extra virgin olive oil

2 garlic cloves, peeled and finely chopped

2 medium hot red chillies, deseeded and finely chopped

2 x 400g tins of chopped tomatoes

3 tablespoons fresh flat-leaf parsley, chopped

500g penne rigate

Salt

1. Heat the oil in a large frying pan over a medium heat and fry the garlic and chilli for about 1 minute, stirring with a wooden spoon.

2. Pour in the chopped tomatoes and parsley, stir well and gently simmer for 15 minutes with the lid off, stirring every couple of minutes. Season with salt, remove from the heat and set aside.

3. Cook the penne in a large saucepan of salted boiling water until al dente. To get the perfect al dente bite, cook the pasta for 1 minute less than instructed on the packet. Once the pasta is cooked, drain and tip back into the same pan it was cooked in.

4. Return the pan of pasta back to a low heat, pour over the spicy tomato sauce and stir all together for 30 seconds to allow the flavours to combine.

5. Serve immediately.

GINO'S TIP: If you don't have fresh chillies, dried chilli flakes work really well too.

Per serving	Kcal	Fat	Saturates	Carbs	Sugars	Fibre	Protein	Salt
	598	13g	2g	98g	10g	8g	18g	0.2g

LINGUINE IN A SOUTHERN ITALIAN SAUCE WITH ANCHOVIES AND CAPERS

There's nothing quite like the taste of a good pasta puttanesca. It's a real Italian classic and, when I'm back in Naples, my mother cooks this for me at least once a week. She always says that it reminds her of my late father – apparently this was the dish they both ordered on their first date. Well, it must have been pretty good – otherwise I wouldn't be here, would I?

SERVES 4

4 tablespoons olive oil
1 garlic clove, peeled and thinly sliced
6 anchovy fillets in oil, drained and chopped
½ teaspoon dried chilli flakes
50g capers in salt, rinsed under cold water
70g pitted Leccino olives in brine or oil, drained and cut in half
1 x 400g tin of cherry tomatoes
400g linguine
Salt

1. Place a large frying pan over a medium heat, add the oil and fry the garlic and anchovies for 2 minutes, stirring occasionally with a wooden spoon.

2. Add the chilli flakes, capers and olives and continue to cook for a further 3 minutes; keep stirring.

3. Pour in the cherry tomatoes, stir well and gently simmer for 8 minutes with the lid off, stirring every couple of minutes. Season with salt, remove from the heat and set aside.

4. Cook the linguine in a large saucepan of salted boiling water until al dente. To get the perfect al dente bite, cook the pasta for 1 minute less than instructed on the packet. Once the pasta is cooked, drain and tip back into the same pan it was cooked in.

5. Pour the puttanesca sauce over the linguine and stir all together for 30 seconds to allow the flavours to combine fully.

6. Serve immediately – without any kind of cheese!

GINO'S TIP: Don't try making this recipe with fresh tomatoes – you need to use tinned tomatoes to get the correct consistency.

Per serving	Kcal	Fat	Saturates	Carbs	Sugars	Fibre	Protein	Salt
	559	15g	2g	84g	6g	8g	17g	2.16g

POTATO DUMPLINGS WITH MOZZARELLA AND FRESH BASIL

There aren't many ingredients here, so you should make sure they're all top quality. When you buy ready-made gnocchi, make sure you check the ingredients list to see how much potato is in them – the best ones will be at least 70 per cent potato. If you buy the really inexpensive varieties, the gnocchi will have an unpleasant floury taste and will be very sticky, so avoid them; you want the best in order to draw out the flavours and textures of this simple, but delicious dish. *Buon appetito!*

SERVES 4

- 3 tablespoons extra virgin olive oil
- 1 onion, peeled and finely chopped
- 1 x 690g bottle of passata (sieved tomatoes)
- 10 fresh basil leaves
- 500g shop-bought plain gnocchi
- 2 x 125g mozzarella balls, drained and cut into small cubes
- Salt and freshly ground black pepper

1. Place a medium saucepan over a medium heat, pour in the oil and fry the onion for 5 minutes until golden. Stir occasionally with a wooden spoon. Pour in the passata and continue to cook for a further 10 minutes, with the lid off, stirring occasionally. Stir in the basil, season with salt and pepper and set aside.

2. Fill a large saucepan three-quarters full with water, add a tablespoon of salt and bring to the boil.

3. Cook the gnocchi in the boiling salted water until they start to float to the top. Drain well and transfer into the pan of tomato and basil sauce.

4. Return the pan to a low heat and cook for 1 minute, stirring to allow the sauce to coat the gnocchi beautifully. Remove from the heat and scatter over the mozzarella. Stir all together for 30 seconds so the mozzarella melts slightly.

5. Serve immediately – ideally with a cold beer!

GINO'S TIP: Gnocchi make a delicious, filling addition to stews and casseroles too.

Per serving	Kcal	Fat	Saturates	Carbs	Sugars	Fibre	Protein	Salt
	452	21g	10g	45g	11g	5g	18g	1.6g

PASTA WITH FETA CHEESE, CHERRY TOMATOES AND FRESH CHIVES

Ever since one fabulous family holiday in Turkey, where feta made a regular appearance at dinner, this cheese has worked its way into loads of my recipes. Here, I really love the contrast between the light, creamy cheese and the juicy, fresh cherry tomatoes. This just sings of summer.

SERVES 4

4 tablespoons extra virgin olive oil

2 garlic cloves, peeled and thinly sliced

150g yellow cherry tomatoes, cut in half

150g red cherry tomatoes, cut in half

400g orecchiette pasta

150g cubed feta cheese in brine or water, drained

3 tablespoons chives, finely chopped

Salt and freshly ground black pepper

1. Place a large frying pan over a medium heat, add the oil and gently fry the garlic and cherry tomatoes for 2 minutes, stirring with a wooden spoon. Season with salt and pepper, remove from the heat and set aside. (Do not cook for longer otherwise the cherry tomatoes will break and you will loose the freshness of the sauce.)

2. Cook the orecchiette in a large saucepan of salted boiling water until al dente. To get the perfect al dente bite, cook the pasta for 1 minute less than instructed on the packet. Once the pasta is cooked, drain and tip back into the same pan it was cooked in.

3. Pour the cherry tomatoes over the pasta with the feta cheese and chives. Mix all together, away from the heat, for 30 seconds to allow all the flavours to combine.

4. Serve immediately.

GINO'S TIP: This is perfect hot or cold – leftovers will make a great packed lunch the next day. Once cooled down to room temperature, keep in a sealed container in the fridge but do not keep for longer than 48 hours.

Per serving	Kcal	Fat	Saturates	Carbs	Sugars	Fibre	Protein	Salt
	594	20g	7g	81g	4g	4g	21g	0.98g

There's nothing better at the end of a long day than a bowlful of goodness. Soups can lift you in the middle of a cold day, be the magic medicine you need when you're hit with a cold or make the perfect lunch to take to work. The best thing about soups and stews? You can prepare them in one pot, so there's minimal washing up and effort. They are also so versatile and are ideal for using up leftovers, transforming cheap cuts of meat or cooking up in bulk for the freezer.

SOUPS & ONE-POTS

SPICY TOMATO AND COUSCOUS SOUP WITH FRESH BASIL

I first made this for lunch when there was hardly anything in the fridge. It's a brilliant recipe for using ingredients you probably already have in your cupboard, plus a few stray fresh veg thrown in. As you can tell, I like my food a little spicy, so the chilli is there to give this a kick while the pesto adds a lovely Italian flavour. Don't be fooled by the tinned ingredients – this is a nutritious feast, low in both fats, a good source of fibre and really filling. Perfect served hot or cold.

SERVES 4

1 tablespoon olive oil
1 large onion, peeled and
  finely chopped
2 large carrots, peeled and
  finely chopped
3 celery sticks, finely
  chopped
1½ teaspoons chilli powder
1 x 400g tin of chopped
  tomatoes
500ml hot vegetable stock
1 x 400g tin of chickpeas,
  drained and rinsed
10 basil leaves, roughly
  chopped, plus a few more
  leaves to garnish
2 tablespoons couscous
Salt

1. Pour the oil into a medium lidded saucepan and place over a medium heat. Fry the onion, carrots and celery for 5 minutes, stirring occasionally with a wooden spoon.

2. Stir in the chilli powder with the tomatoes, stock and chickpeas and chopped basil. Bring to the boil, then reduce the heat to low, cover with a lid and simmer for 30 minutes, stirring every 10 minutes or so.

3. Add the couscous. Season with salt, stir and continue to cook for a further 5 minutes with the lid on.

4. Ladle into bowls and garnish with a few basil leaves on top.

GINO'S TIP: This soup won't reheat well with the couscous in because the grains will become soggy if overcooked. If you want to get ahead on this soup or freeze it, follow the recipe up to the end of step 3, then cool and refrigerate or freeze. Add the couscous grains when reheating.

Per serving	Kcal 215	Fat 6g	Saturates 1g	Carbs 28g	Sugars 12g	Fibre 9g	Protein 8g	Salt 0.5g

CHUNKY SPLIT PEA AND HAM SOUP

This is classic comfort food; it's filling, hearty and inexpensive and uses only five ingredients. Home-made stock is the base for many traditional Italian dishes; here it's made by boiling the gammon with onions and herbs for a really deep flavour. Don't add any salt to this; the gammon is already quite salty.

SERVES 4

375g smoked gammon joint
2 large onions, peeled and
    left whole
1 bay leaf
300g green split peas, rinsed
    thoroughly
Freshly ground black pepper

1. Put the gammon, onions, bay leaf and 1.5 litres cold water into a medium lidded saucepan. Bring to the boil. Skim off and discard the white scum that rises to the surface, then reduce the heat to low and simmer with the lid on for 1¼ hours. Stir occasionally with a wooden spoon.

2. Add the split peas and continue to cook for a further 45 minutes, then remove from the heat.

3. Remove the bay leaf and discard. Transfer the onions and 1 ladleful of the liquid to a jug or bowl. Using a hand-held blender, blitz to a smooth purée. Pour back into the soup and stir to combine.

4. Remove the gammon and pull into bite-sized pieces, discarding any fat. Return the meat back to the soup. Give it a good stir and return to the heat to warm through.

5. Ladle the soup into bowls. Season with black pepper and serve immediately with thin slices of toasted garlic bread (see page 73)

GINO'S TIP: The longer you cook the peas, the more they will break down and the smoother the puréed soup will be.

Per serving	Kcal	Fat	Saturates	Carbs	Sugars	Fibre	Protein	Salt
	487	13g	4g	47g	9g	17g	37g	2.84g

MUTTON CASSEROLE WITH RED WINE AND ROOT VEGETABLES

Mutton has had a rather unfair reputation as being a stringy, unappetising meat from an old animal, but the truth is that it's massively underrated – when cooked properly, it's full of flavour and is melt-in-the-mouth delicious. Mutton is meat from an animal that's usually over two years old and is much cheaper to buy than lamb. It needs long, slow cooking to be at its best, making it ideal for casseroles. I love making this for my family; I can leave it cooking while we head out to the park before coming home to a hot tasty meal.

SERVES 4

3 tablespoons olive oil
500g diced mutton
1 tablespoon tomato purée
50ml red wine
500ml hot beef stock
1 tablespoon fresh rosemary leaves
2 bay leaves
1 onion, peeled and sliced
1 large carrot, peeled and cut into 1cm discs
1 parsnip, peeled and cut into 1cm discs
½ swede, peeled and cut into 1cm chunks
1 turnip, cut into 1cm chunks
Salt and freshly ground black pepper

1. Preheat the oven to 140°C/gas mark 1.

2. Pour half the oil into a medium lidded, flameproof casserole and place over a medium heat. Add the mutton and fry for 5 minutes, stirring occasionally with a wooden spoon to make sure that the meat is brown on all sides. Add the tomato purée, stir and continue to cook for 2 minutes. Pour in the wine and allow the alcohol to cook off for 1 minute. Stir in the stock with the rosemary and bay leaves. Cover the dish with a lid and transfer to the oven for 1 hour.

3. Meanwhile, pour the remaining oil into a medium saucepan and place over a medium heat. Fry the onion, carrots, parsnip, swede and turnip for 5 minutes, stirring occasionally with a wooden spoon.

4. Transfer the vegetables to the casserole and season with salt and pepper. Cover and return to the oven for a further 2 hours, stirring occasionally, or until the meat is very tender.

5. Serve with creamy mash and a green vegetable of your choice.

GINO'S TIP: Mutton is not always easy to find in the supermarkets, but if you make friends with your local butcher, they should be able to get you some.

Per serving	Kcal	Fat	Saturates	Carbs	Sugars	Fibre	Protein	Salt
	437	28g	10g	13g	10g	8g	27g	0.6g

SPICY RED LENTIL AND CARROT SOUP

When you need a soup in a hurry, this is the perfect recipe – It can be put together quickly from store cupboard ingredients and makes a filling and low-fat lunch or light supper. If you like, double up the quantities and put half in the freezer for another day. Why not take some to work tomorrow?

SERVES 4

2 tablespoons olive oil
1 large onion, peeled and
  finely chopped
2 large carrots, peeled and
  finely chopped
3 garlic cloves, peeled and
  finely chopped
1 litre hot vegetable stock
100g dried red lentils, rinsed
  thoroughly
½ teaspoon hot paprika
10g fresh flat-leaf
parsley, roughly chopped
Salt

1. Pour the oil into a medium saucepan and place over a medium heat. Add the onion and carrots and fry for 3 minutes, stirring occasionally with a wooden spoon. Add the garlic and cook for 2 minutes, stirring occasionally.

2. Pour in the hot stock with the lentils and paprika and bring to the boil. Reduce the heat to low, cover with a lid and simmer for 15 minutes or until the lentils are tender. Transfer 2 ladlefuls of soup to a jug and using a hand-held blender, blitz until smooth. Pour back into the soup, season with salt and stir to heat through.

3. Ladle into bowls, sprinkle over the parsley and serve.

GINO'S TIP: Lentils are a fantastic storecupboard standby. Once opened, put them in an airtight container and they will keep indefinitely, although for best flavour and texture, eat them within one year.

Per serving	Kcal	Fat	Saturates	Carbs	Sugars	Fibre	Protein	Salt
	232	7g	1g	29g	8g	7g	11g	0.7g

STUFATO DI POLLO E FUNGHI

CHICKEN AND MUSHROOM CASSEROLE

This is a fantastic warming dish for autumn and is so easy to put together and leave bubbling away in the oven. Minimum cooking, minimum washing up! Chicken thighs are a cheap and delicious cut, adding extra flavour and juiciness – especially if you buy them with the bone in. Curl up on the sofa with this, your partner, some good red wine and crusty bread… *perfetto!*

SERVES 4

30g plain flour
4 skinless chicken thighs, about 750g in total
2 tablespoons vegetable oil
2 red onions, peeled and thinly sliced
2 garlic cloves, peeled and thinly sliced
2 large potatoes, peeled and cut into 1cm cubes
3 carrots, peeled and cut into 5mm discs
150g chestnut mushrooms, thinly sliced
1 tablespoon fresh thyme leaves
2 bay leaves
1 tablespoon tomato purée
500ml hot chicken stock
Salt and freshly ground black pepper

1. Preheat the oven to 190°C/gas mark 5.

2. Put the flour onto a large flat plate and generously season with salt and pepper. Coat the chicken pieces with the seasoned flour; discard the leftover flour.

3. Pour the oil into a large lidded, flameproof casserole and place over a medium heat. Add the chicken and fry in the oil for 10 minutes, turning halfway through. Do not move the chicken around in the pan between turning as you want it to take on some colour. Remove the chicken from the casserole with a slotted spoon and set aside.

4. Add the onions to the casserole and fry for 2 minutes, scraping the bottom of the dish with a wooden spoon to de-glaze. Add the garlic, potatoes, carrots, mushrooms, thyme and bay leaves and stir all together.

5. Stir the tomato purée into the chicken stock and pour it over the vegetables. Give it a good stir and season with salt and pepper. Return the chicken pieces to the casserole dish together with any juices.

6. Cover the casserole dish with a lid and transfer into the oven for 1 hour, stirring halfway through.

GINO'S TIP: Serve the casserole immediately – ideally with a bottle of Cannonau red wine.

Per serving	Kcal 458	Fat 12g	Saturates 2g	Carbs 36g	Sugars 11g	Fibre 8g	Protein 48g	Salt 0.8g

WHITE FISH MINESTRONE WITH CHICKPEAS

Minestrone is a fantastic way to pack loads of vegetables into one meal. There are no rules on which particular vegetables you should use, so it's brilliant for using up any veg you happen to have in the fridge. It also makes a great base for other ingredients: you can mix it up to suit your mood or your own personal tastes, for instance, by adding pasta, or some leftover cooked chicken, by swapping the chickpeas for cannellini or borlotti beans, or by just adding your favourite veg. I think fish is a great addition to this soup; it almost becomes a delicious light stew.

SERVES 4

2 tablespoons olive oil
2 leeks, white part only, thinly sliced
2 carrots, peeled and thinly sliced
2 courgettes, trimmed and thinly sliced
100g green beans, cut into 1cm pieces
1 x 400g tin of chickpeas, drained and rinsed
1 litre hot chicken stock
200g white fish fillets, cut into 4 pieces (cod or pollock work perfectly)
Salt and white pepper

1. Pour the oil into a large saucepan and place over a medium heat. Add the leeks, carrots, courgettes and green beans and fry for 10 minutes, stirring occasionally with a wooden spoon.

2. Add the chickpeas and chicken stock and bring to the boil, then reduce the heat to a simmer. Season the fish well with salt and pepper and place in the pan, poking the fish gently until it is fully submerged under the cooking liquid. Poach for 8 minutes or until the fish is cooked through.

3. Carefully lift out the fish pieces and place one in each bowl. Ladle the soup over the top, season with pepper and serve immediately.

GINO'S TIP: Always buy fish as fresh as possible. Frozen fillets are also a good standby. If you buy fish that's been reduced in price, eat it within 24 hours or freeze it immediately after purchase.

Per serving	Kcal	Fat	Saturates	Carbs	Sugars	Fibre	Protein	Salt
	259	9g	1g	16g	6g	10g	24g	0.8g

CREAMY CHICKEN SOUP WITH BASIL PESTO

This is a really simple chicken soup – but with a Gino-style Italian twist. The pesto adds a delicious extra flavour to this warming bowl of goodness. It's a great source of protein and the perfect comfort food after a long day or when you're feeling the chill. If anyone in my family is fighting a bug, I'm in the kitchen making them this – it's like medicine in a mug!

SERVES 4

80g salted butter
1 red onion, peeled and thinly sliced
300g skinless chicken breast, cut into strips
1 large carrot, peeled and cut into 5mm cubes
1 large potato, peeled and cut into 5mm cubes
1 leek, thinly sliced
1 tablespoon tomato purée
60g plain flour
1.2 litres hot chicken stock
1 tablespoon ready-made basil pesto

1. Melt 20g of the butter in a large saucepan over a medium heat. Add the onion and chicken and fry for 5 minutes, stirring occasionally with a wooden spoon. Add the carrot and potato and continue to cook for a further 5 minutes, stirring occasionally. Add the leek and tomato purée, give it a good stir and cook for a further 3 minutes. Remove from the heat and set aside.

2. Melt the remaining butter in a medium saucepan over a medium heat. When the butter starts to bubble, tip in the flour and stir continuously for 3 minutes with a wooden spoon. Reduce the heat to medium-low and gradually pour in the chicken stock a little at a time, stirring continuously. Do not add more stock until the last amount has been incorporated. This should take about 10 minutes.

3. Pour the thickened stock into the pan with the vegetables and chicken. Stir in the pesto and bring to the boil, then reduce the heat and simmer for 15 minutes.

4. Serve hot. *Buon appetito!*

GINO'S TIP: For the most nutritious chicken broth, boil up a chicken carcass after a Sunday lunch with a few leftover vegetables to make a really fresh, fabulous-flavoured stock. You can then freeze it in portions.

Per serving	Kcal	Fat	Saturates	Carbs	Sugars	Fibre	Protein	Salt
	426	20g	11g	28g	6g	6g	31g	1.3g

SUPER SIMPLE ROOT VEGETABLE CASSEROLE WITH PAPRIKA AND HONEY

I know what you carnivores are thinking – a casserole with no meat? Well, in many parts of Italy, people grow up on dishes like this; beans are used in almost everything to create a satisfying and inexpensive meal. So trust me, this will give you all the goodness your body needs and leave you feeling full.
Give it a go – I promise you'll love it!

SERVES 4

2 red onions, peeled and sliced
½ swede, peeled and cut into 2cm chunks
2 parsnips, peeled and cut into 2cm chunks
250g Chantenay carrots, topped and tailed and sliced lengthways
200g celeriac, peeled and cut into 2cm chunks
1 tablespoon tomato purée
1 tablespoon runny honey
500ml hot vegetable stock
1 teaspoon hot paprika
1 x 400g tin of chopped tomatoes
1 x 400g tin of cannellini beans, drained
3 tablespoons chives, chopped
Salt and freshly ground black pepper

1. Preheat the oven to 180°C/gas mark 4.

2. Put the onions, swede, parsnips, carrots and celeriac into a large lidded casserole. Stir the tomato purée and honey into the vegetable stock and pour it over the vegetables. Add the paprika, tinned tomatoes and beans and stir all together. Season with salt and pepper.

3. Put the lid on the casserole and transfer to the oven for 1½ hours, stirring halfway through.

4. Remove from the oven and stir in the chives. Check the seasoning and serve immediately with warm crusty bread.

Per serving	Kcal	Fat	Saturates	Carbs	Sugars	Fibre	Protein	Salt
	231	2g	0.2g	35g	22g	16g	9g	0.6g

FENNEL AND BEAN CASSEROLE WITH CRISPY BREADCRUMBS

The flavour of fennel is much more appreciated in Italy than it is over here. We eat this vegetable raw or cooked – and it tastes so different depending on how you prepare it. Eaten raw, it is crisp and mildly anise-flavoured – when cooked, however, it loses its crispness and really cranks up the aniseed! Long cooking gets the best out of fennel, so here it is boiled then baked in the classic Italian way.

SERVES 4

2 tablespoons olive oil
2 red onions, peeled and
  finely chopped
1 x 400g tin of cannellini
  beans, drained
1 head of celery, thinly sliced
  (including the central
  leaves)
2 fennel bulbs, cored and
  thinly sliced
2 tablespoons tomato purée
2 teaspoons dried oregano
1 teaspoon fresh thyme
  leaves
1 vegetable stock cube
2 x 400g tins of chopped
  tomatoes
5 slices of stale bread,
  blitzed into breadcrumbs
  in a food processor
Salt and freshly ground black
  pepper

1. Pour the oil into a medium lidded, flameproof casserole and place over a medium heat. Fry the onions for 5 minutes, stirring occasionally with a wooden spoon.

2. Add the beans, celery, fennel, tomato purée, 1 teaspoon of the oregano, the thyme, vegetable stock cube and tinned tomatoes. Stir all together to combine and season with salt and pepper. Bring to the boil, then reduce the heat, cover and simmer for half an hour, stirring occasionally.

3. Preheat the oven to 200°C/gas mark 6.

4. Mix the breadcrumbs with the remaining oregano and scatter over the vegetables. Put the casserole, uncovered, in the oven for 20–25 minutes or until the breadcrumbs are golden brown. Serve immediately.

GINO'S TIP: Fennel is at its best and in season between June and September – which also means it will be at its cheapest! Buy the smaller, young bulbs if you can, as they are more tender and taste better.

Per serving	Kcal	Fat	Saturates	Carbs	Sugars	Fibre	Protein	Salt
	290	8g	1g	37g	16g	13g	12g	1.28g

SIMPLE PEA SOUP WITH FRESH MINT AND LEMON ZEST

Laced with fresh herbs and packing a citrus punch, this soup is summer in a bowl. Frozen peas are one of the best standbys you can have in your kitchen. They are frozen within hours of being picked, so they're packed with nutrients and they have a really fantastic bright green colour.

SERVES 4

25g salted butter
2 tablespoons olive oil
1 onion, peeled and finely chopped
1 large potato, peeled and finely chopped
2 celery sticks, thinly sliced
1 litre hot vegetable stock
350g frozen peas, defrosted
Grated zest of 1 unwaxed lemon
20g fresh mint leaves
100g low-fat mascarpone cheese
Salt and freshly ground black pepper

1. Put the butter and oil into a medium saucepan and place over a medium heat. Add the onion, potato and celery and fry for 5 minutes, stirring occasionally with a wooden spoon.

2. Pour in the stock, stir and bring to the boil. Reduce the heat and simmer for 10 minutes until the potatoes are tender. Stir occasionally. Add the peas and lemon zest and gently cook for a further 5 minutes.

3. Remove from the heat, add the mint leaves and, using a hand-held blender, blitz until smooth. Bring back to the boil and season with salt and pepper.

4. Ladle into bowls and top each bowl with a spoonful of mascarpone. Grind over some extra black pepper and serve immediately.

GINO'S TIP: If you prefer a bit of texture in your soup, leave the vegetables a little chunky when you blend them.

Per serving	Kcal	Fat	Saturates	Carbs	Sugars	Fibre	Protein	Salt
	309	17g	8g	25g	10g	8g	10g	0.8g

RICE & PULSES

In Italy, rice usually means risotto. One of our most famous foodie exports is Arborio risotto rice, to which you can add all sorts of different ingredients to make the ultimate comfort food. You can glam it up for entertaining or keep it simple for all the family. When cooked, risotto rice provides a creamy texture but without the heavy calories. Pulses are another popular component of the Italian diet; packed with protein, they can replace meat in stews or casseroles, or bulk out the meat component to make a cheaper dish. You'll even find beans in one of the risotto recipes that follow!

CREAMY BUTTERNUT SQUASH AND ASPARAGUS RISOTTO

This is the kind of dish that makes you think you're being really indulgent, but in actual fact it's healthier than most risottos. That's because here the delicious creaminess comes from the non-fattening butternut squash, which softens during the cooking and adds a sweetness to the risotto. A fabulous seasonal dish, perfect at the end of a long summer when the nights get shorter.

SERVES 4

4 tablespoons olive oil
1 large onion, peeled and
   finely chopped
350g Arborio rice
50ml white wine
250g butternut squash,
   peeled and chopped
   into 1cm cubes
2 sprigs of thyme, leaves
   stripped and chopped
1 litre hot vegetable stock
   (made with stock cubes)
125g asparagus tips
   (chopped the same size
   as the squash)
25g salted butter, at room
   temperature
40g freshly grated
   Parmesan cheese
Salt and freshly ground
   black pepper

1. Pour the oil into a medium saucepan and fry the onion over a medium heat for 3 minutes, stirring occasionally with a wooden spoon.

2. Add the rice and fry for 2 minutes allowing the rice to toast into the hot oil. Stir continuously with a wooden spoon. Pour in the wine and continue to cook for a further minute.

3. Stir in the squash and thyme. Pour in a couple of ladles of stock and bring to a simmer. Continue to cook and stir until all the stock is absorbed. Pour in the rest of the stock a little at the time, cooking until each addition is absorbed. Once the rice has begun to swell add the asparagus.

4. When the rice is cooked and the squash is soft, take the saucepan off the heat and add the butter and Parmesan cheese. Quickly stir all together for 30 seconds until the risotto becomes creamy. Season with salt and pepper and serve immediately.

GINO'S TIP: Asparagus is expensive to buy out of season, so if your budget won't stretch to it, replace the spears with some sage leaves fried in a little olive oil.

Per serving	Kcal 580	Fat 21g	Saturates 7g	Carbs 80g	Sugars 9g	Fibre 4g	Protein 14g	Salt 0.94g

NEAPOLITAN RICE SALAD

This is a really satisfying salad. Packed with a rainbow of fresh and preserved ingredients, it is as colourful as it is delicious – not to mention nutritious. It's quick to assemble, but it really does need the 2 hours sitting in the fridge to get all those flavours working together – so plan ahead on this one. Of course, that also means that it's a great choice if you want to impress everyone by producing a delicious lunch out of nowhere for the next day . . .

SERVES 6

400g American-style long-grain rice
100g frozen peas, defrosted
100g green beans, cut into 2cm pieces
100g pitted green olives in brine, drained and cut in half
100g pickled small gherkins, chopped into small pieces
1 red pepper, deseeded and chopped into small pieces
3 tablespoons shop-bought mayonnaise
3 tablespoons extra virgin olive oil
10 yellow cherry tomatoes, cut into quarters
8 hard-boiled eggs
Salt and freshly ground black pepper
60g freshly shaved Parmesan cheese, to serve

1. Half-fill a large saucepan with water, add 1 tablespoon of salt and bring to the boil. Cook the rice until al dente, stirring occasionally. Add the peas and beans and continue to cook for a further 2 minutes. Rinse under cold running water for 1 minute, drain well and tip into a large bowl. The cooking time may vary, depending on the quality of the rice – check the packet instructions.

2. Gently fold all the remaining ingredients into the bowl except for the Parmesan cheese and the hard-boiled eggs. Season with salt and pepper, mix well and cover with cling film. Put in the fridge for 2 hours to allow the flavours to combine properly; give the mixture a stir every 30 minutes.

3. Take the rice out of the fridge 20 minutes before you want to serve it. Transfer the rice salad onto a large serving plate. Peel and quarter the hard-boiled eggs and arrange over the salad, then scatter over the shavings of Parmesan cheese.

GINO'S TIP: Always cool rice as quickly as possible – ideally within 1 hour – to prevent the bacteria that could cause food poisoning from forming. Rinsing with cold water helps to do this, as does spreading it out on a cold plate. Do not put rice in the fridge until cold.

Per serving	Kcal	Fat	Saturates	Carbs	Sugars	Fibre	Protein	Salt
	554	27g	4g	58g	3g	4g	17g	1.69g

THREE BEANS, TUNA AND RED ONION ON WARM GARLIC BREAD

To many Italians this classic dish is a starter, usually served as an antipasto, but I think it's just too good for that and should take centre stage. It's really healthy and fresh, but if there's any left over it keeps well for a packed lunch the next day.

SERVES 4

1 x 400g tin of chickpeas, drained and rinsed

1 x 400g tin of red kidney beans, drained and rinsed

1 x 400g tin of butter beans, drained and rinsed

1 large red onion, peeled and finely sliced

10 red cherry tomatoes, cut into quarters

Juice of ½ lemon

4 tablespoons extra virgin olive oil

2 tablespoons fresh mint leaves, chopped

8 thin slices of crusty bread

1 garlic clove, peeled and halved

2 x 160g tins of tuna in spring water, drained

Salt and freshly ground black pepper

1. Put the chickpeas, kidney beans and butter beans into a large bowl with the sliced onion and cherry tomatoes.

2. Squeeze over the lemon juice and pour in the extra virgin olive oil. Add the mint and season with salt and pepper. Mix all together and leave to rest for 10 minutes at room temperature. After 5 minutes stir all together to allow the flavours to combine properly.

3. Toast the bread on both sides and rub each slice with the cut side of the garlic. Place each slice of bread in the middle of a serving plate.

4. Gently fold the tuna into the beans and then pile on top of the warm garlic bread. Fantastic served with a cold beer.

GINO'S TIP: This dish can be thrown together using any beans you have in the cupboard – substitute whatever you have (but not baked beans!).

Per serving	Kcal	Fat	Saturates	Carbs	Sugars	Fibre	Protein	Salt
	505	16g	2g	25g	7g	14g	30g	0.9g

RISOTTO WITH CHICORY, SAGE AND ASPARAGUS

Now this is a risotto for a special occasion. It has great flavours and textures from the chicory and asparagus and, when combined with the lightly warmed (but not softened) cherry tomatoes, all the ingredients add an exciting bit of bite against the creamy risotto rice. You must try this dish – I guarantee it will be a success!

SERVES 4

4 tablespoons olive oil

1 large onion, peeled and finely chopped

6 large fresh sage leaves, finely sliced

400g Arborio rice

50ml white wine

1.2 litres hot vegetable stock (made with stock cubes)

250g chicory, trimmed with leaves roughly sliced

100g asparagus tips, cut into 2cm pieces

10 red cherry tomatoes, cut into quarters

35g salted butter, at room temperature

40g freshly grated Grana Padano cheese

Salt and freshly ground black pepper

1. Pour the oil into a medium heavy-based saucepan, place over a medium heat and fry the onion and sage for 4 minutes. Stir occasionally with a wooden spoon.

2. Add the rice and fry for 3 minutes allowing the rice to toast in the oil. Stir continuously with a wooden spoon. Pour in the wine and continue to cook for a further minute to allow the alcohol to evaporate.

3. Pour in a couple of ladles of stock and bring to a simmer. Continue to cook and stir until all the stock is absorbed. At this point please stay with the saucepan because you need to keep stirring with a wooden spoon. Add the chicory and pour in the rest of the stock, a little at the time, cooking until each addition is absorbed. It will take between 15–17 minutes and you may not need to add all the stock. Add the asparagus tips to the risotto about 7 minutes before the end of the cooking time.

4. Once the rice is cooked, take the saucepan off the heat and add the cherry tomatoes with the butter and the Grana Padano cheese.

5. Stir all together for 30 seconds to allow the risotto to become creamy. The risotto shouldn't be too thick; you want it to ooze. Season with salt and pepper and serve immediately.

GINO'S TIP: When buying chicory, look for crisp, yellow-tipped leaves – avoid using those with green tips, as they will be very bitter.

Per serving	Kcal	Fat	Saturates	Carbs	Sugars	Fibre	Protein	Salt
	640	23g	8g	88g	8g	4g	14g	1.1g

CHUNKY TOMATO AND BORLOTTI BEAN CASSEROLE

In Italy we use a lot of pulses in our cooking; they are a cheap, nutritious ingredient that will pack out a meal and help you to feel full for longer. If you use tinned tomatoes as well as tinned beans, this recipe makes a fantastic storecupboard standby to whip up quickly when hunger strikes. It's fantastic any time of year, but particularly good when the weather gets cold. And personally, I can't resist mopping up with some warm garlic bread.

SERVES

600g plum tomatoes
3 tablespoons olive oil
1 large red onion, peeled
    and roughly chopped
130g diced pancetta
600ml hot vegetable stock
    (made with stock cubes)
2 teaspoons smoked paprika
2 teaspoons caster sugar
1 tablespoon cornflour
1 tablespoon balsamic
    vinegar
1 x 400g tin of borlotti beans,
    drained
3 tablespoons fresh flat-leaf
    parsley, chopped
Salt and freshly ground black
    pepper

1. With a sharp knife score the tomatoes all the way around the middle and plunge into boiling water for 2 minutes. Drain and transfer to a bowl of cold water for 2 minutes. Peel away the skin and discard, roughly chop the flesh and set aside.

2. Pour the oil into a medium saucepan and fry the onion and pancetta over a medium heat for 5 minutes. Stir occasionally with a wooden spoon.

3. Add the tomatoes together with the stock, paprika and sugar. Bring to the boil then reduce the heat and simmer, without the lid, for 15 minutes.

4. Put the cornflour into a small bowl and mix to a paste with the balsamic vinegar. Stir into the soup together with the beans and continue to cook for a further 5 minutes, stirring occasionally. Stir in the parsley, season with salt and pepper and continue to cook for 5 minutes.

5. Ladle into serving bowls and serve immediately with a few slices of warm garlic bread.

GINO'S TIP: If you don't have any borlotti beans, cannellini beans make a good replacement.

Per serving	Kcal 340	Fat 20g	Saturates 7g	Carbs 23g	Sugars 12g	Fibre 8g	Protein 12g	Salt 1.3g

SPICY BEAN STEW WITH SPINACH

I love any kind of stew. Mostly I like ones with meat that I can cook long and slow, but this speedy vegetarian version is also a winner. Healthy and hearty, it's packed with vegetables and has a warming kick from the chilli. A real feast in a bowl, it's cheap yet really satisfying.

SERVES 4

1 tablespoon olive oil
1 large onion, peeled and
  finely chopped
½ teaspoon dried chilli
  flakes
½ teaspoon smoked paprika
1 x 400g tin of chopped
  tomatoes
1 teaspoon caster sugar
200ml hot vegetable stock
  (made with stock cubes)
1 x 400g tin of cannellini
  beans, drained
120g green beans, washed
  and roughly chopped
100g fresh spinach leaves,
  roughly chopped
Salt

1. Pour the oil into a medium saucepan and fry the onion and chilli flakes over a medium heat for 5 minutes. Stir occasionally with a wooden spoon. Add the paprika and cook for a further minute.

2. Pour in the tomatoes, sugar and stock. Bring to the boil then reduce the heat and simmer gently for 10 minutes, uncovered. Stir occasionally.

3. Add the cannellini beans and green beans and cook for a further 5 minutes, stirring occasionally.

4. Finally, add the spinach and cook for 5 minutes longer. Season with salt and serve hot with a few slices of garlic bread.

GINO'S TIP: Make sure you wash the spinach and drain it well and never wash spinach leaves before storing in the fridge or they will go soggy.

Per serving	Kcal	Fat	Saturates	Carbs	Sugars	Fibre	Protein	Salt
	152	4g	1g	18g	10g	8g	8g	0.2g

AUTUMN-INSPIRED RISOTTO WITH MUSHROOMS AND FRESH THYME

Mushrooms are a passion in Italy; in some areas you even need a licence to gather them in the wild. Among the wild mushrooms, porcini are king and because they are so prized, they can be quite expensive. However, their intense, earthy flavour means you don't need many to make an impact. Here I've also used chestnut mushrooms to make this a feast of fungi!

SERVES 4

10g sliced dried porcini
  mushrooms
4 tablespoons olive oil
1 large onion, peeled and
  finely chopped
250g chestnut mushrooms,
  sliced
1 tablespoon fresh thyme
  leaves
350g Arborio rice
50ml dry white wine

1. Soak the dried porcini mushrooms in a small bowl of cold water for 30 minutes.

2. Pour the olive oil into a medium saucepan and fry the onion over a medium heat for 4 minutes, stirring occasionally with a wooden spoon. Meanwhile drain the soaked porcini mushrooms and squeeze out any excess water.

3. Add all the mushrooms with the thyme to the onions and continue to cook for a further 3 minutes, stirring occasionally. Add the rice and stir continuously for 3 minutes, allowing the rice to toast in the olive oil and begin to absorb all the mushroom and thyme flavours.

1.2 litres hot vegetable stock (made with stock cubes)

25g salted butter, at room temperature

40g freshly grated Parmesan cheese

Salt and freshly ground black pepper

4. Pour in the wine and continue to cook for 2 minutes allowing the alcohol to evaporate. Keep stirring. Start to add the stock a little at a time, stirring occasionally, allowing the rice to absorb the stock before adding more. (If you need extra liquid, use hot water.)

5. After about 20 minutes, when most of the stock has been absorbed, remove the saucepan from the heat and stir the butter into the risotto. It is very important that you stir the butter very fast into the rice for at least 30 seconds – this creates a fantastic creamy texture.

6. Finally stir in the Parmesan cheese, season with salt and pepper and serve immediately.

GINO'S TIP: For a stronger mushroom flavour, add the mushroom soaking liquid to the stock and use to cook the risotto.

Per serving	Kcal	Fat	Saturates	Carbs	Sugars	Fibre	Protein	Salt
	569	21g	7g	77g	6g	3g	14g	1.1g

OOZING RISOTTO WITH SEARED KING PRAWNS AND LEMON

The most simple of seafood risottos, yet so elegant. Lemons are a popular pairing with seafood in Italy, especially along the Amalfi coast, where the landscape is covered with trees groaning with these brightly coloured fruits. I'm not being biased, but the crops in this area are known as among the best in the world. Although you might not be able to get Sorrento lemons, get the best ingredients you can find for a real taste of the Med.

SERVES 4

12 large frozen prawns,
  defrosted for at least
  8 hours in the fridge
4 tablespoons olive oil
2 shallots, peeled and finely
  chopped
350g Arborio rice
50ml Italian dry white wine
1 litre hot fish stock (made
  with stock cubes)
Grated zest and juice of
  1 unwaxed lemon
2 tablespoons fresh flat-leaf
  parsley, chopped
50ml semi-skimmed milk
50g salted butter
Salt and white pepper

1. Wash the prawns under cold water and thoroughly dry with kitchen paper. Set aside.

2. Pour the oil into a medium saucepan and place over a medium heat. Add the shallots and fry for 4 minutes, stirring occasionally with a wooden spoon. Add the rice and stir for 1 minute to coat the grains in the hot oil.

3. Pour in the wine and continue to cook for a further minute to allow the alcohol to evaporate. Pour in a couple of ladles of stock and bring to a simmer. Continue to cook and stir until all the stock is absorbed. At this point please stay with the saucepan because you need to keep stirring with a wooden spoon.

4. Pour in the rest of the stock, a little at the time, cooking until each addition is absorbed. It will take between 15 and 17 minutes and you may not need to add all the stock.

5. Once the rice is cooked, take the saucepan off the heat and stir in the lemon zest and juice, parsley and milk. Stir all together for 30 seconds until the risotto becomes shiny and creamy. Season with salt and white pepper and set aside while you cook the prawns.

6. Put the butter into a large frying pan and place over a high heat. Season the prawns with salt and pepper and place in the pan. Fry for 2 minutes on each side; do not move the prawns while they are cooking as you want them to get a nice sear and to brown all over.

7. Serve the risotto on warm plates and arrange the seared prawns on top.

Per serving	Kcal	Fat	Saturates	Carbs	Sugars	Fibre	Protein	Salt
	597	23g	8g	70g	3g	1g	24g	1.3g

CREAMY RISOTTO WITH CHICKEN, PEAS AND BASIL PESTO

If you're one of those people who finds the whole idea of risotto really scary, try this one. It is the easiest recipe to put together, using ingredients you may already have in the cupboard or freezer. The secret to a really good risotto is stirring, stirring, stirring. It takes a little time and attention, but the result is so worth it! And if you don't devour the whole thing at dinner, this is great for lunch the next day.

SERVES 4

2 tablespoons olive oil
1 large onion, peeled and finely chopped
1 large skinless chicken breast (about 200g), diced into small cubes
350g Arborio rice
1.2 litres hot vegetable stock (made with stock cubes)
100g frozen peas, defrosted
65g ready-made basil pesto
35g salted butter, at room temperature
40g freshly grated Grana Padano cheese
Salt and freshly ground black pepper

1. Place a medium heavy-based saucepan over a medium heat, pour in the oil and fry the onion for 4 minutes, stirring occasionally with a wooden spoon. Add the diced chicken and continue to fry for a further 2 minutes.

2. Add the rice and fry for 2 minutes, allowing the rice to toast in the hot oil. Stir continuously with a wooden spoon.

3. Pour in a couple of ladles of stock and bring to a simmer. Continue to cook and stir until all the stock is absorbed. At this point please stay with the saucepan because you need to keep stirring with a wooden spoon. Stir in the peas.

4. Pour in the rest of the stock, a little at the time, cooking until each addition is absorbed. It will take between 15 and 17 minutes and you may not need to add all the stock.

5. Once the rice is cooked, take the saucepan off the heat and add the pesto, butter and Grana Padano cheese. Quickly stir all together for 30 seconds until the risotto turns creamy.

6. Season with salt and pepper and serve immediately; this is perfect with a bottle of chilled Vermentino white wine.

GINO'S TIP: For the perfect risotto, soften the onions but don't let them brown, as this will destroy the flavour of the dish; the same goes for the rice – browning the grains locks in the starch, which you want to release to get the creamy texture.

Per serving	Kcal	Fat	Saturates	Carbs	Sugars	Fibre	Protein	Salt
	649	25g	9g	78g	8g	4g	26g	1.5g

SIMPLE CHICKEN AND SAFFRON RISOTTO WITH FRESH ROSMARY

This has got to be the simplest risotto; only a few ingredients, but all carefully selected for maximum impact. Saffron is the most expensive spice in the world, but it won't break the budget as you just need the tiniest amount for it to add its sweet flavour and vibrant yellow colour.

SERVES 4

½ teaspoon saffron threads
1.2 litres hot vegetable stock (made with stock cubes)
3 tablespoons olive oil
1 large onion, peeled and finely chopped
1 large skinless chicken breast (about 200g), cut into small cubes
1 tablespoon fresh rosemary leaves, finely chopped
400g Arborio rice
50ml white wine
35g salted butter, at room temperature
40g freshly grated Grana Padano cheese
Salt and white pepper

1. Mix the saffron with 4 tablespoons of hot stock in a small bowl and set aside (see Gino's tip below).

2. Place a medium heavy-based saucepan over a medium heat, pour in the oil and fry the onion for 2 minutes, stirring occasionally with a wooden spoon. Add the chicken and rosemary and continue to fry for a further 2 minutes.

3. Add the rice and fry for 3 minutes to allow the rice to toast into the hot oil. Stir continuously with a wooden spoon. Pour the wine over the rice and continue to cook for a further minute until the alcohol evaporates.

4. Pour over the saffron mixture and stir. Pour in a couple of ladles of stock and bring to a simmer. Continue to cook and stir until all the stock is absorbed. At this point please stay with the saucepan because you need to keep stirring with a wooden spoon.

5. Pour in the rest of the stock, a little at the time, cooking until each addition is absorbed. It will take between 15 and 17 minutes and you may not need to add all the stock.

6. Once the rice is cooked, take the saucepan off the heat and add the butter and Grana Padano cheese. Stir all together for 30 seconds until the risotto becomes creamy.

7. Season with salt and white pepper and serve immediately.

GINO'S TIP: To get a really strong flavour and colour from the saffron, leave it to soak for about 30 minutes before using it. Don't buy yellow saffron threads as they won't be the real thing – the best ones are a deep red with orange tips.

Per serving	Kcal 642	Fat 21g	Saturates 8g	Carbs 85g	Sugars 6g	Fibre 3g	Protein 25g	Salt 1.17g

RISOTTO WITH SMOKED SALMON, LEMON AND CHIVES

Smoked salmon? Sounds expensive, but you'd be surprised. This is the perfect dish for a dinner party where you want to impress, but also stay within a budget. It also makes an easy midweek indulgence any time of year.

SERVES 4

3 tablespoons olive oil
1 large onion, peeled and finely chopped
350g Arborio rice
50ml white wine
1.2 litres hot fish stock (made with stock cubes)
35g salted butter, at room temperature
4 tablespoons chives, chopped
Juice of 1 unwaxed lemon
10 yellow cherry tomatoes, cut into quarters
100g smoked salmon, roughly chopped
Salt and freshly ground black pepper

1. Pour the oil into a medium heavy-based saucepan, place over a medium heat and fry the onion for 3 minutes until soft but not browned. Stir occasionally with a wooden spoon.

2. Add the rice and fry for 3 minutes to allow the rice to toast into the hot oil. Stir continuously with a wooden spoon. Pour the wine over the rice and continue to cook for a further minute to allow the alcohol to evaporate.

3. Pour in a couple of ladles of stock and bring to a simmer. Continue to cook and stir until all the stock is absorbed. At this point please stay with the saucepan because you need to keep stirring with a wooden spoon.

4. Pour in the rest of the stock, a little at the time, cooking until each addition is absorbed. It will take between 15–17 minutes and you may not need to add all the stock.

5. Once the rice is cooked, take the saucepan off the heat and add the butter, chives, lemon juice, tomatoes and smoked salmon. Stir all together for 30 seconds until the risotto becomes creamy and all the ingredients are fully combined.

6. Season with salt and pepper and serve immediately. Don't be tempted to add any kind of cheese on top; you will ruin the fresh flavours of the smoked salmon and lemon juice.

Per serving	Kcal 606	Fat 19g	Saturates 6g	Carbs 76g	Sugars 6g	Fibre 2g	Protein 29g	Salt 1.79g

RISOTTO WITH MINCED PORK, ROSEMARY AND BORLOTTI BEANS

We use borlotti beans a lot in Italian cooking, either dried or fresh. These raw beans have a beautiful pinky-brown marbled colour, which is sadly lost when they are cooked. But they do have a fantastic flavour and add a little bit of sweetness, making this a wonderfully rich risotto without being heavy. Serve it with Parmesan shavings for a little extra indulgence.

SERVES 4

3 tablespoons olive oil
1 large onion, peeled and finely chopped
250g lean pork mince
1 tablespoon fresh rosemary leaves, finely chopped
300g Arborio rice
50ml white wine
1 litre hot vegetable stock (made with stock cubes)
35g salted butter, at room temperature
1 x 400g tin of borlotti beans, drained
40g freshly grated Parmesan cheese
Salt and freshly ground black pepper

1. Pour half the oil into a medium heavy-based saucepan, place over a medium heat and fry the onion for 1 minute until soft but not browned. Stir with a wooden spoon. Add the minced meat with the rosemary and continue to fry for a further 5 minutes, stirring occasionally with a wooden spoon. Use a slotted spoon to remove the meat and onion from the pan and set aside.

2. Pour the remaining oil into the saucepan and add the rice. Fry for 3 minutes over a medium heat to allow the rice to toast in the flavoured hot oil. Stir continuously with a wooden spoon.

3. Pour the wine over the rice and continue to cook for a further minute until the alcohol evaporates. Pour in a couple of ladles of stock and bring to a simmer. Continue to cook and stir until all the stock is absorbed. At this point please stay with the saucepan because you need to keep stirring with a wooden spoon.

4. Pour in the rest of the stock, a little at the time, cooking until each addition is absorbed. It will take between 15 and 17 minutes and you may not need to add all the stock.

5. Once the rice is cooked, take the saucepan off the heat, add the butter, borlotti beans, the cooked minced meat and grated Parmesan cheese. Gently stir all together for 30 seconds until the risotto becomes creamy and all the ingredients are fully combined.

6. Season with salt and pepper and serve immediately.

GINO'S TIP: If you have bought fresh rosemary in a packet, you can freeze leftover stems by chopping the leaves then adding them to ice-cube trays and topping them up to cover with either olive oil or water. Then you can just pop out the ready chopped leaves as needed!

Per serving	Kcal	Fat	Saturates	Carbs	Sugars	Fibre	Protein	Salt
	632	23g	9g	72g	6g	6g	29g	1.14g

RISOTTO WITH COURGETTES, ROASTED PEPPERS AND YELLOW CHERRY TOMATOES

This is a great hit for your 5-a-day and is colourful, light and delicious too. I love roasted peppers in jars – they are a real time-saver rather than having to make your own – so I always have them in the cupboard. They have a great flavour and can be added to so many different recipes or just eaten along with some antipasti. This is the kind of dish I'd consider turning vegetarian for . . .

SERVES 4

4 tablespoons olive oil
1 large red onion, peeled and finely chopped
4 tablespoons fresh flat-leaf parsley, chopped
350g Arborio rice
50ml white wine
1.2 litres hot vegetable stock (made with stock cubes)
2 courgettes, trimmed and cut into 1cm cubes
1 x 280g jar roasted peppers in brine, drained and roughly sliced
50g salted butter, at room temperature
10 yellow cherry tomatoes, cut in half
50g freshly grated Pecorino cheese
Salt and freshly ground black pepper

1. Pour the oil into a medium heavy-based saucepan, place over a medium heat and fry the onion and parsley for 2 minutes, stirring occasionally with a wooden spoon.

2. Add the rice and fry for 2 minutes to allow the rice to toast in the hot oil. Stir continuously with a wooden spoon. Pour the wine over the rice and continue to cook for a further minute until the alcohol evaporates.

3. Pour in a couple of ladles of stock and bring to a simmer. Continue to cook and stir until all the stock is absorbed. At this point please stay with the saucepan because you need to keep stirring with a wooden spoon.

4. Add the courgettes and then pour in the rest of the stock, a little at the time, cooking until each addition is absorbed. It will take between 15 and 17 minutes and you may not need to add all the stock. Add the peppers to the risotto 3 minutes before the end of the cooking time.

5. Once the rice is cooked, take the saucepan off the heat and add the butter with the cherry tomatoes and the Pecorino cheese. Stir all together for 30 seconds until the risotto becomes creamy – it should not be too thick, you want it to ooze.

6. Season with salt and pepper and serve immediately.

Per serving	Kcal	Fat	Saturates	Carbs	Sugars	Fibre	Protein	Salt
	639	28g	11g	79g	7g	4g	14g	1.4g

PIZZA

No Italian cookery book is complete without a chapter on pizza – one of my favourite dishes. Pizzas are so easy to make and when it comes to toppings, almost anything goes. They are great for using up leftovers and if you prep ahead and put some home-made dough in the freezer, they make the ultimate healthy fast food, too.

CLASSIC NEAPOLITAN THIN CRUST PIZZA WITH MOZZARELLA AND FRESH BASIL

This classic Italian pizza was created on my home patch and that may be part of the reason why I love pizza so much – it was a regular feature on the D'Acampo menu when I was growing up and it's still a favourite with my own family. This is considered a 'pure' pizza by some Italians and, although being Neapolitan I'm a bit biased, I think this is still one of the best.

MAKES 2 (TO SERVE 4)

2 tablespoons extra virgin olive oil, plus extra for brushing
200g strong white flour, plus extra for dusting
1 x 7g sachet fast-action (easy blend) dried yeast
140ml warm water
2 x 125g mozzarella balls, drained and cut into small cubes
10 large basil leaves
1 x 400g tin of chopped tomatoes
Salt and freshly ground black pepper

1. Brush 2 medium baking trays with oil and set aside.

2. Put the flour, yeast and a pinch of salt into a large bowl, make a well in the centre and pour in the water and extra virgin olive oil. Mix to create a wet dough (use the handle of a wooden spoon so you don't get sticky fingers).

3. Turn the dough onto a clean, well-floured surface and work it with your hands for about 5 minutes until smooth and elastic. Shape the dough into 2 balls and place in the centre of the oiled baking trays. Brush the tops of the dough balls with a little oil and cover with cling film. Leave to rest at room temperature for 30 minutes.

4. Preheat the oven to 210°C/gas mark 7.

5. Once rested and still in the baking trays, use your fingertips to push each dough ball out from the centre, creating 2 round discs about 22cm in diameter.

6. Pour the chopped tomatoes equally over the middle of each pizza base and spread evenly, leaving a 1cm border clean from the tomatoes. The best way to do this is to pour the tomatoes into the middle and spread outwards using the back of a tablespoon.

7. Sprinkle a pinch of salt and pepper over each pizza. Scatter the mozzarella evenly over the tomatoes and bake in the middle of the oven for 15 minutes, until golden and crisp. Scatter the basil leaves over the top 1 minute before the end of the cooking time.

8. Serve hot and enjoy with a cold beer!

GINO'S TIP: Always use really fresh basil for this pizza – the dried stuff simply won't do.

Per serving	Kcal	Fat	Saturates	Carbs	Sugars	Fibre	Protein	Salt
	419	19g	9g	41g	4g	3g	19g	0.8g

SUPER-SPICY PIZZA TOPPED WITH SPICY SALAMI

This is the pizza for when the boys come round to watch football. I like to use a spicy salami that has a real kick (no pun intended), but you can go as hot as you can handle! I'm a real fan of heat, so I like to pep it up even more with a good dash of chilli flakes. It's so easy to put together and washes down really well with a cold bottle of beer. 'Back of the Net', as we say in Italy!

MAKES 2 (TO SERVE 4)

2 tablespoons extra virgin olive oil, plus extra for brushing
200g strong white flour, plus extra for dusting
1 x 7g sachet fast-action (easy blend) dried yeast
140ml warm water
1 x 400g tin of chopped tomatoes
1 teaspoon dried chilli flakes
2 tablespoons fresh flat-leaf parsley, chopped
1 red pepper, deseeded and very thinly sliced
1 x 125g mozzarella ball, drained and cut into small cubes
10 slices of spicy salami
Salt

1. Brush 2 medium baking trays with oil and set aside.

2. Put the flour, yeast and a pinch of salt into a large bowl, make a well in the centre and pour in the water with the extra virgin olive oil. Mix to create a wet dough (use the handle of a wooden spoon so you don't get sticky fingers).

3. Turn the dough onto a clean, well-floured surface and work it with your hands for about 5 minutes until smooth and elastic. Shape the dough into 2 balls and place in the centre of the oiled baking trays. Brush the tops of the dough balls with a little oil and cover with cling film. Leave to rest at room temperature for 30 minutes.

4. Meanwhile, pour the tomatoes into a medium bowl and stir in the chilli flakes and parsley. Season with a little salt and set aside while you preheat the oven to 210°C/gas mark 7.

5. Once rested and still in the baking trays, use your fingertips to push each dough ball out from the centre, creating 2 round discs about 22cm in diameter.

6. Pour the spicy tomato mixture equally over the middle of each pizza base and spread evenly, leaving a 1cm border clean from the tomatoes. The best way to do this is to pour the tomato mixture into the middle and spread outwards using the back of a tablespoon.

7. Sprinkle over the pepper slices, then scatter the mozzarella evenly over the peppers and lay the salami on top. Bake in the middle of the oven for 15 minutes, until golden and crisp. Serve hot with a cold beer.

GINO'S TIP: This is a great pizza for the morning after the football, too!

Per serving	Kcal	Fat	Saturates	Carbs	Sugars	Fibre	Protein	Salt
	406	18g	7g	43g	6g	4g	17g	0.9g

TRADITIONAL SOUTHERN ITALIAN PIZZA WITH GARLIC, OLIVE OIL AND CHILLIES

This traditional pizza is topped with the perfect marriage of ingredients – creamy mascarpone plus a spicy kick of garlic and chilli. They are so good together. Mascarpone is a bit of treat ingredient, so here I've used a light version to keep the fat content down. But there's no compromise on flavour – you'll love it!

MAKES 2 (TO SERVE 4)

4 tablespoons extra virgin olive oil, plus extra for brushing
200g strong white flour, plus extra for dusting
1 x 7g sachet fast-action (easy blend) dried yeast
140ml warm water
250g light mascarpone cheese
3 garlic cloves, peeled and finely chopped
1 large hot red chilli, deseeded and finely chopped
2 tablespoons fresh flat-leaf parsley, chopped
Salt

1. Brush 2 medium baking trays with oil and set aside.

2. Put the flour, yeast and a pinch of salt into a large bowl, make a well in the centre and pour in the water with 2 tablespoons of the extra virgin olive oil. Mix to create a wet dough (use the handle of a wooden spoon so you don't get sticky fingers).

3. Turn the dough onto a clean, well-floured surface and work it with your hands for about 5 minutes until smooth and elastic. Shape the dough into 2 balls and place in the centre of the oiled baking trays. Brush the tops of the dough balls with a little oil and cover with cling film. Leave at room temperature to rest for 30 minutes.

4. Meanwhile, prepare the topping. Put the mascarpone cheese into a medium bowl and stir in the garlic, chilli and parsley. Pour in the remaining 2 tablespoons of oil with 2 tablespoons of warm water, season with salt and stir all together. Set aside at room temperature while you preheat the oven to 210°C/gas mark 7.

5. Once rested and still in the baking trays, use your fingertips to push each dough ball out from the centre, creating 2 round discs about 22cm in diameter.

6. Evenly spread the mascarpone mixture over the pizza bases and bake in the middle of the oven for 15 minutes, until golden and crisp.

7. Serve hot with a crispy salad of your choice.

Per serving	Kcal	Fat	Saturates	Carbs	Sugars	Fibre	Protein	Salt
	443	25g	11g	41g	2g	2g	12g	0.1g

SPICY PIZZA TOPPED WITH ANCHOVIES AND GARLIC

The Marinara and the Margherita are considered by traditional Italian restaurants, such as Da Michele pizzeria in Via C. Sersale in Naples, to be the 'true' pizzas. Now normally I wouldn't mess with that – but I like a bit of spice in my life, so I've added a bit of chilli to heat it up. I'm Italian, and I'm from Naples – I'm allowed …

MAKES 2 (TO SERVE 4)

2 tablespoons extra virgin olive oil, plus extra for brushing
200g strong white flour, plus extra for dusting
1 x 7g sachet fast-action (easy blend) dried yeast
140ml warm water
1 x 400g tin of chopped tomatoes
2 garlic cloves, peeled and thinly sliced
1 teaspoon dried oregano
1 teaspoon dried chilli flakes
8 anchovy fillets in oil, drained
8 pitted black olives in brine, drained and cut in half
Salt

1. Brush 2 medium baking trays with oil and set aside.

2. Put the flour, yeast and a pinch of salt into a large bowl, make a well in the centre and pour in the water with 2 tablespoons of extra virgin olive oil. Mix to create a wet dough (use the handle of a wooden spoon so you don't get sticky fingers).

3. Turn the dough onto a clean, well-floured surface and work it with your hands for about 5 minutes until smooth and elastic. Shape the dough into 2 balls and place in the centre of the oiled baking trays. Brush the tops of the dough balls with a little oil and cover with cling film. Leave at room temperature to rest for 30 minutes.

4. Meanwhile, pour the tomatoes into a medium bowl and stir in the garlic, oregano and chilli flakes. Season with a little salt and set aside while you preheat the oven to 210°C/gas mark 7.

5. Once rested and still in the baking trays, use your fingertips to push each dough ball out from the centre, creating 2 round discs about 22cm in diameter.

6. Pour the tomato mixture equally over the middle of each pizza base and spread evenly, leaving a 1cm border clean from the tomatoes. The best way to do this is to pour the tomatoes in the middle and spread outwards using the back of a tablespoon.

7. Scatter the anchovies and olives over the pizzas and bake in the middle of the oven for 15 minutes, until golden and crisp. Serve hot.

GINO'S TIP: This pizza is quite salty; if you want to reduce the saltiness of the anchovies, soak the fillets in a little milk before using.

Per serving	Kcal 563	Fat 15g	Saturates 2g	Carbs 83g	Sugars 8g	Fibre 6g	Protein 20g	Salt 2.59g

PIZZA WITH BASIL PESTO AND THREE DIFFERENT TOMATOES

This is essentially a Margherita with a twist – but what a twist! The secret to success here lies in getting the right ingredients. There aren't very many, so it's worth spending the budget on getting the freshest, most flavoursome tomatoes and the best-quality pesto that you can. It will make such a difference.

MAKES 2 (TO SERVE 4)

2 tablespoons extra virgin olive oil, plus extra for brushing

200g strong white flour, plus extra for dusting

1 x 7g sachet fast-action (easy blend) dried yeast

140ml warm water

1 x 400g tin of chopped tomatoes

2 tablespoons ready-made basil pesto

10 red cherry tomatoes, cut into quarters

10 yellow cherry tomatoes, cut into quarters

40g freshly shaved Parmesan cheese

Salt and freshly ground black pepper

1. Brush 2 medium baking trays with oil and set aside.

2. Put the flour, yeast and a pinch of salt into a large bowl, make a well in the centre and pour in the water and extra virgin olive oil. Mix to create a wet dough (use the handle of a wooden spoon so you don't get sticky fingers).

3. Turn the dough onto a clean, well-floured surface and work it with your hands for about 5 minutes or until smooth and elastic. Shape the dough into 2 balls and place in the centre of the oiled baking trays. Brush the tops of the dough balls with a little oil and cover with cling film. Leave at room temperature to rest for 30 minutes.

4. Meanwhile, pour the tomatoes into a medium bowl and stir in the basil pesto. Season with a little salt and pepper and set aside while you preheat the oven to 210°C/gas mark 7.

5. Once rested and still in the baking trays, use your fingertips to push each dough ball out from the centre, creating two round discs about 22cm in diameter.

6. Pour the tomato mixture equally over the middle of each pizza base and spread evenly, leaving a 1cm border clean from the tomatoes. The best way to do this is to pour the tomatoes into the middle and spread outwards using the back of a tablespoon.

7. Scatter the cherry tomatoes over the pizzas and bake in the middle of the oven for 15 minutes, until golden and crispy. Scatter over the Parmesan shavings and serve immediately.

GINO'S TIP: Don't let the toppings sit on the pizza base for too long before cooking, otherwise the dough will become soggy.

Per serving	Kcal	Fat	Saturates	Carbs	Sugars	Fibre	Protein	Salt
	613	19g	3g	88g	11g	7g	18g	0.6g

PIZZA WITH MUSHROOMS AND GREEN OLIVES

If you're new to making pizza, this is the one to start with – it's so simple. I love this combination of mushrooms and olives as it is full of earthy, salty flavours, but without the high salt count.

MAKES 2 (TO SERVE 4)

4 tablespoons extra virgin olive oil, plus extra for brushing

200g strong white flour, plus extra for dusting

1 x 7g sachet fast-action (easy blend) dried yeast

140ml warm water

1 x 400g tin of chopped tomatoes

2 garlic cloves, peeled and thinly sliced

1 teaspoon dried oregano

120g chestnut mushrooms, sliced

10 pitted green olives in brine, drained and cut in half

Salt and freshly ground black pepper

1. Brush 2 medium baking trays with oil and set aside.

2. Put the flour, yeast and a pinch of salt into a large bowl, make a well in the centre and pour in the water with 2 tablespoons of the extra virgin olive oil. Mix to create a wet dough (use the handle of a wooden spoon so you don't get sticky fingers).

3. Turn the dough onto a clean, well-floured surface and work it with your hands for about 5 minutes until smooth and elastic. Shape the dough into 2 balls and place in the centre of the oiled baking trays. Brush the tops of the dough balls with a little oil and cover with cling film. Leave at room temperature to rest for 30 minutes.

4. Meanwhile, pour the tomatoes into a medium bowl and stir in the garlic and oregano. Season with a little salt and pepper and set aside while you preheat the oven to 210°C/gas mark 7.

5. Prepare the mushrooms: pour the remaining oil into a small frying pan and fry the mushrooms for 5 minutes over a medium heat, season and stir occasionally. Set aside.

6. Once rested and still in the baking trays, use your fingertips to push each dough ball out from the centre, creating 2 round discs about 22cm in diameter.

7. Pour the tomato mixture equally over the middle of each pizza base and spread evenly, leaving a 1cm border clean from the tomatoes. The best way to do this is to pour the tomatoes into the middle and spread outwards using the back of a tablespoon.

8. Scatter the mushrooms and olives over the pizzas and bake in the middle of the oven for 15 minutes, until golden and crisp. Enjoy.

GINO'S TIP: To prevent the base going soggy, make sure you preheat your oven properly before you bake the pizza. That way the base will be nice and crisp.

Per serving	Kcal	Fat	Saturates	Carbs	Sugars	Fibre	Protein	Salt
	647	25g	4g	84g	8g	6g	18g	0.8g

LARGE PIZZA WITH CRISPY PANCETTA AND CARAMELISED ONIONS

This is where the crispy home-made base really comes into its own, making the perfect bed for the crispy, salty pancetta and creamy, sweet caramelised onions. The recipe originally came from the Alsace region, where it is known as tarte flambée. The North Italian version uses white onions, but red onions apparently started to be substituted as people realised they don't leave the same oniony smell on the breath! So this is a delicious pizza that won't ruin your date night!

MAKES 1 LARGE PIZZA
(TO SERVE 4)

3 tablespoons extra virgin olive oil, plus extra for brushing
200g strong white flour, plus extra for dusting
1 x 7g sachet fast-action (easy blend) dried yeast
140ml of warm water plus 2 tablespoons
70g diced pancetta
2 large red onions, peeled and thinly sliced
1 teaspoon brown sugar
2 x 125g mozzarella balls, drained and cut into small cubes
Salt and freshly ground black pepper

1. Brush a large baking tray with oil and set aside.

2. Put the flour, yeast and a pinch of salt into a large bowl, make a well in the centre and pour in 140ml of warm water with 2 tablespoons of the extra virgin olive oil. Mix to create a wet dough (use the handle of a wooden spoon so you don't get sticky fingers).

3. Turn the dough onto a clean, well-floured surface and work it with your hands for about 5 minutes until smooth and elastic. Shape the dough into a ball and place in the centre of the oiled baking tray. Brush the top of the dough ball with a little oil and cover with cling film. Leave at room temperature to rest for 30 minutes.

4. Meanwhile, pour the remaining tablespoon of extra virgin olive oil into a medium saucepan and place over a medium heat. Fry the pancetta with the onions for 8 minutes, stirring occasionally with a wooden spoon. Add the sugar and 2 tablespoons of warm water and continue to cook for 3 minutes. Set aside at room temperature while you preheat the oven to 210°C/gas mark 7.

5. Once rested and still in the baking tray, use your fingertips to push the dough ball out from the centre, creating a rectangular shape about 45cm long and 20cm wide.

6. Scatter the onion mixture over the pizza base and the mozzarella on top. Sprinkle with lots of black pepper and bake in the middle of the oven for 15 minutes, until golden and crispy.

7. Serve immediately with a bottle of chilled Italian white wine.

GINO'S TIP: For perfect caramelised onions you need the heat low and slow. If they look like they are drying out, add a little more water, but only a little – you don't want them in too much liquid.

Per serving	Kcal	Fat	Saturates	Carbs	Sugars	Fibre	Protein	Salt
	539	27g	13g	48g	8g	4g	23g	1.2g

NEAPOLITAN STUFFED FOLDED PIZZA WITH MOZZARELLA, RICOTTA AND SALAMI

Calzone literally translated means 'pair of trousers' – how that became the name for a folded pizza, I just don't know! What I do know is that this stuffed pizza originated in my home region of Naples. Different regions in Italy have their own version of this 'sandwich', but this is a traditional Neapolitan one, with home-made dough encasing the classic combination of mozzarella, ricotta and salami. It's perfect for lunch on the go!

MAKES 2 (TO SERVE 4)

2 tablespoons extra virgin olive oil, plus extra for brushing

200g strong white flour, plus extra for dusting

1 x 7g sachet fast-action (easy blend) dried yeast

140ml warm water

1 x 400g tin of chopped tomatoes

150g ricotta cheese

1 x 125g mozzarella ball, drained and cut into small cubes

10 basil leaves

10 slices of salami Napoli

Salt and freshly ground black pepper

1. Brush 2 medium baking trays with oil and set aside.

2. Put the flour, yeast and a pinch of salt into a large bowl, make a well in the centre and pour in the water and extra virgin olive oil. Mix to create a wet dough (use the handle of a wooden spoon so you don't get sticky fingers).

3. Turn the dough onto a clean, well-floured surface and work it with your hands for about 5 minutes until smooth and elastic. Shape the dough into 2 balls and place in the centre of the oiled baking trays. Brush the tops of the dough balls with a little oil and cover with cling film. Leave at room temperature to rest for 30 minutes.

4. Meanwhile, pour the tomatoes into a medium bowl, season with a little salt and pepper and set aside. Transfer 3 tablespoons of the tomato mixture to a small bowl (you will need this to brush the folded pizzas before cooking), then preheat the oven to 210°C/gas mark 7.

5. Once rested and still in the baking trays, use your fingertips to push each dough ball out from the centre, creating 2 round discs about 22cm in diameter.

6. Spread the tomatoes equally over just half the surface of each pizza base using the back of a tablespoon. Leave a 1cm border clean from the tomatoes. Scatter the ricotta, mozzarella and basil over the tomatoes and lay the salami on top. Fold the empty half of each base over to enclose the filling. Pinch the edges to seal and turn inwards, making tucks at regular intervals, to create a rope-like effect.

7. Brush the top of each calzone with the reserved tomatoes and bake in the middle of the oven for 15 minutes, until golden and crisp.

GINO'S TIP: Calzone is a fantastic way of using up any leftover veg, bits of ham or cheese that you have in your fridge – be creative!

Per serving	Kcal	Fat	Saturates	Carbs	Sugars	Fibre	Protein	Salt
	447	22g	10g	42g	5g	2g	20g	0.9g

MINI PIZZAS WITH FOUR DIFFERENT TOPPINGS

These pizzette are the perfect solution when you have guests over, or when no one can agree on what to put on a large pizza to share. These are just suggestions; you can add whatever else you like to customise the little pizze to suit everyone's different tastes. I really wanted to show that a pizza doesn't always have to be the size of a vinyl LP; it can be whatever you want it to be.

MAKES 4

2 tablespoons extra virgin olive oil, plus extra for brushing
200g strong white flour, plus extra for dusting
1 x 7g sachet fast-action (easy blend) dried yeast
140ml warm water
1 x 400g tin of chopped tomatoes
2 x 125g reduced-fat mozzarella balls, drained and cut into small cubes
Dried chilli flakes
2 slices of cooked ham, cut into strips
4 yellow cherry tomatoes, cut into quarters
Salt

1. Brush 2 large baking trays with oil and set aside. Put the flour, yeast and a pinch of salt into a large bowl, make a well in the centre and pour in the water and extra virgin olive oil. Mix to create a wet dough (use the handle of a wooden spoon so you don't get sticky fingers).

2. Turn the dough onto a clean, well-floured surface and work it with your hands for about 5 minutes until smooth and elastic. Shape the dough into 4 balls and place 2 balls on each oiled baking tray, leaving a distance of 15cm between each ball. Brush the tops of the dough balls with a little oil and cover with cling film. Leave to rest at room temperature for 30 minutes, while you preheat the oven to 210°C/gas mark 7.

3. Once rested and still in the baking trays, use your fingertips to push each dough ball out from the centre, creating 2 round discs about 10cm in diameter on each baking tray. Pour the tinned tomatoes equally over the middle of 3 of the pizza bases and spread evenly, leaving a ½ cm border clean from the tomatoes. The best way to do this is to pour the tomatoes into the middle and spread outwards using the back of a tablespoon.

4. Scatter the mozzarella evenly over all 4 pizza bases. You should have 3 pizzas with tomato and mozzarella and 1 with only mozzarella. Scatter half of the ham over the pizza base with only mozzarella and sprinkle over a few chilli flakes. Scatter the remaining ham over 1 of the other pizzas. Arrange the cherry tomatoes over 1 of the remaining 2 pizzas. You should now have 1 pizza with mozzarella, ham and chilli, 1 with mozzarella and tomato, 1 with mozzarella, tomato and ham, 1 with mozzarella and cherry tomatoes.

5. Bake in the middle of the oven for 13 minutes. Serve while still hot.

Per serving	Kcal 388	Fat 13g	Saturates 6g	Carbs 43g	Sugars 5g	Fibre 3g	Protein 22g	Salt 0.87g

GLUTEN-FREE FLORENCE-STYLE THIN CRUST PIZZA WITH EGGS AND SPINACH

There's now no reason why coeliacs or those with gluten intolerance can't enjoy a proper home-made pizza. This fantastic gluten-free base is made with fresh ingredients, so you know exactly what is in it – and it takes no more time to prepare than a traditional wheat-based version. The classic Florentine topping of spinach, eggs and cheese makes this one of the healthiest pizzas you can make and it's a real favourite in my family. Of course, once you've perfected the base, you can top it with whatever you like!

MAKES 2 (TO SERVE 4)

2 tablespoons extra virgin
    olive oil, plus extra for
    brushing
200g gluten-free flour, plus
    extra for dusting
1 x 7g sachet fast-action
    (easy blend) dried yeast
140ml warm water
200g frozen spinach,
    defrosted
2 x 125g mozzarella balls,
    drained and cut into
    small cubes
2 really fresh eggs
Salt and freshly ground black
    pepper

1. Brush 2 medium baking trays with oil and set aside.

2. Put the flour, yeast and a pinch of salt into a large bowl, make a well in the centre and pour in the water with the extra virgin olive oil. Mix to create a wet dough (use the handle of a wooden spoon so you don't get sticky fingers).

3. Turn the dough onto a clean, well-floured surface and work it with your hands for about 5 minutes until smooth and elastic. Shape the dough into 2 balls and place in the centre of the oiled baking trays. Brush the tops of the dough balls with a little oil and cover with cling film. Leave at room temperature to rest for 30 minutes.

4. Meanwhile, squeeze the spinach between your hands to remove any excess water, roughly chop and set aside. Preheat the oven to 210°C/gas mark 7.

5. Once rested and still in the baking trays, use your fingertips to push each dough ball out from the centre, creating two round discs about 22cm in diameter. Scatter the mozzarella and spinach equally over the middle of each pizza base, leaving a border of 1cm at the edges and an empty 5cm circle in the centre.

6. Sprinkle a pinch of salt and pepper over each pizza, then bake in the middle of the oven for 7 minutes. Remove the trays from the oven and crack an egg into the centre of each pizza. Return to the oven to bake for a further 8 minutes. Enjoy with a bottle of full-bodied Italian red wine.

GINO'S TIP: Gluten-free dough can be stickier than wheat-based dough, so you may need more of the extra gluten-free flour than usual when kneading and shaping it.

Per serving	Kcal 388	Fat 13g	Saturates 6g	Carbs 43g	Sugars 5g	Fibre 3g	Protein 22g	Salt 0.87g

PIZZA TOPPED WITH SMOKED SALMON AND CAPERS

Growing up in Naples, smoked salmon was something we only ate on special occasions because it was so expensive. Now it is much cheaper, especially if you use trimmings, and should be eaten more often as it is a great source of Omega 3 acids. Smoked salmon has a strong flavour and so can take the sharpness of the capers – and you won't need much extra salt because the salmon and capers are already quite salty.

MAKES 2 (TO SERVE 4)

2 tablespoons extra virgin olive oil, plus extra for brushing

200g strong white flour, plus extra for dusting

1 x 7g sachet fast-action (easy blend) dried yeast

140ml warm water

2 tablespoons capers in brine

1 x 400g tin of chopped tomatoes

2 garlic cloves, peeled and thinly sliced

1 teaspoon dried oregano

100g smoked salmon, roughly sliced

Salt and freshly ground black pepper

1. Brush 2 medium baking trays with oil and set aside.

2. Put the flour, yeast and a pinch of salt into a large bowl, make a well in the centre and pour in the water and extra virgin olive oil. Mix to create a wet dough (use the handle of a wooden spoon so you don't get sticky fingers).

3. Turn the dough onto a clean, well-floured surface and work it with your hands for about 5 minutes until smooth and elastic. Shape the dough into 2 balls and place in the centre of the oiled baking trays. Brush the tops of the dough balls with a little oil and cover with cling film. Leave at room temperature to rest for 30 minutes.

4. Meanwhile, rinse the capers under cold running water, drain and pat dry with kitchen paper. Roughly chop and set aside. Pour the tomatoes into a medium bowl and stir in the garlic and oregano. Season with a little pepper and set aside while you preheat the oven to 210°C/gas mark 7.

5. Once rested and still in the baking trays, use your fingertips to push each dough ball out from the centre, creating 2 round discs about 22cm in diameter.

6. Pour the tomato mixture equally over the middle of each pizza base and spread evenly, leaving a 1cm border clean from the tomatoes. The best way to do this is to pour the tomatoes in the middle and spread outwards using the back of a tablespoon.

7. Scatter the salmon and capers over the pizzas and bake in the middle of the oven for 15 minutes. Serve hot with a crisp green salad dressed with lemon juice and a little extra virgin olive oil.

Per serving	Kcal	Fat	Saturates	Carbs	Sugars	Fibre	Protein	Salt
	618	17g	3g	84g	8g	6g	29g	1.9g

LARGE SHARING PIZZA WITH GOAT'S CHEESE AND ROCKET LEAVES

Peppery fresh rocket and creamy goat's cheese is such a delicious combination and one that's popular as a salad – but trust me, it works really well on a pizza too! It looks fantastic, with the red, white and vibrant green. In fact, it's the Italian flag on a plate!

MAKES 1 (TO SERVE 4)

2 tablespoons extra virgin olive oil, plus extra for brushing
200g strong white flour, plus extra for dusting
1 x 7g sachet fast-action (easy blend) dried yeast
140ml warm water
1 x 400g tin of chopped tomatoes
1 x 125g reduced-fat mozzarella ball, drained and cut into small cubes
125g goat's cheese
70g rocket leaves
Salt and freshly ground black pepper

1. Brush a large baking tray with oil and set aside.

2. Put the flour, yeast and a pinch of salt into a large bowl, make a well in the centre and pour in the water and extra virgin olive oil. Mix to create a wet dough (use the handle of a wooden spoon so you don't get sticky fingers).

3. Turn the dough onto a clean, well-floured surface and work it with your hands for about 5 minutes until smooth and elastic. Shape the dough into a ball and place in the centre of the oiled baking tray. Brush the top of the dough ball with a little oil and cover with cling film. Leave at room temperature to rest for 30 minutes while you preheat the oven to 210°C/gas mark 7.

4. Once rested and still in the baking tray, use your fingertips to push the dough ball out from the centre, creating a rectangular shape about 45cm long and 20cm wide.

5. Pour the chopped tomatoes in the middle of the pizza base and spread evenly, leaving a 1cm border clean from the tomatoes. The best way to do this is to pour the tomatoes into the middle and spread outwards using the back of a tablespoon.

6. Sprinkle a pinch of salt and pepper over the pizza. Scatter the mozzarella and goat's cheese evenly over the tomatoes and bake in the middle of the oven for 15 minutes, until golden and crispy.

7. Serve hot with the rocket leaves scattered on top.

GINO'S TIP: Use a goat's cheese that has a good flavour and is not too mild; it needs to stand up to the other flavours, in particular the peppery rocket.

Per serving	Kcal	Fat	Saturates	Carbs	Sugars	Fibre	Protein	Salt
	417	18g	9g	42g	5g	3g	21g	0.79g

PIZZA WITH COURGETTES AND BALSAMIC GLAZE

I love grilled courgettes, but sometimes it's just a hassle to prepare them, particularly if I'm hungry and need feeding right now! Here I can get the same flavour and texture by simply tossing them on top of this fantastic pizza. It looks amazing with all the overlapping circles of cheese and courgette – a real showstopper.

MAKES 2 (TO SERVE 4)

2 tablespoons extra virgin olive oil, plus extra for brushing

200g strong white flour, plus extra for dusting

1 x 7g sachet fast-action (easy blend) dried yeast

140ml warm water

1 large courgette

2 x 125g reduced-fat mozzarella balls, drained and cut into small cubes

2 tablespoons fresh flat-leaf parsley, chopped

4 tablespoons balsamic glaze

Salt and freshly ground black pepper

1. Brush 2 medium baking trays with oil and set aside.

2. Put the flour, yeast and a pinch of salt into a large bowl, make a well in the centre and pour in the water and extra virgin olive oil. Mix to create a wet dough (use the handle of a wooden spoon so you don't get sticky fingers).

3. Turn the dough onto a clean, well-floured surface and work it with your hands for about 5 minutes until smooth and elastic. Shape the dough into 2 balls and place in the centre of the oiled baking trays. Brush the tops of the dough balls with a little oil and cover with cling film. Leave at room temperature to rest for 30 minutes.

4. Meanwhile, trim and discard the top and bottom of the courgette. With a sharp knife cut the courgette into really thin discs, or use a mandolin if you have one, as it will make this job much easier. Set aside while you preheat the oven to 210°C/gas mark 7.

5. Once rested and still in the baking trays, use your fingertips to push each dough ball out from the centre, creating two round discs about 22cm in diameter.

6. Scatter the mozzarella evenly over the pizza bases and sprinkle the parsley on top. Lay the courgette discs over the mozzarella and parsley slightly overlapping, creating a circle effect. Sprinkle a pinch of salt and pepper over each pizza.

7. Bake in the middle of the oven for 15 minutes, until golden and crispy. Drizzle over the balsamic glaze and serve immediately.

GINO'S TIP: For a really crispy pizza base, slide the pizza tin on top of a preheated baking tray in the oven.

Per serving	Kcal	Fat	Saturates	Carbs	Sugars	Fibre	Protein	Salt
	439	19g	10g	47g	9g	2g	19g	0.8g

MEAT

I'm a self-confessed meat lover, but it can be a very expensive ingredient – so this chapter is full of recipes that will keep the carnivores happy without breaking the budget. From ideas for the long, slow cooking of cheaper cuts of meat until they become mouth-wateringly tender to recipes for simple dishes using more costly cuts with fabulously filling vegetables or pulses, there are meals for every occasion and season here.

STUFFED CHICKEN BREASTS WITH GARLIC AND MINT MASCARPONE

Mint and garlic isn't a combination that immediately comes to mind, but it really works! For anyone who thinks that chicken breasts are tasteless, all I can say is – try this. Mascarpone features a lot in Northern Italian cooking, being a cheese that is a speciality of Lombardy, but its fat content is quite high, so here I've used a light mascarpone that is lower in fat but still has the flavour and creaminess I want for this dish. The best thing about this? You can do all the prep in the morning so it's ready to stick in the oven when hunger calls.

SERVES 4

200g reduced-fat
  mascarpone cheese
2 garlic cloves, peeled and
  crushed
10 fresh mint leaves, finely
  chopped
4 skinless chicken breasts
100ml hot chicken stock
  (made from stock cubes)
Salt and freshly ground black
  pepper

1. Preheat the oven to 180°C/gas mark 4.

2. Put the mascarpone, garlic and mint into a small bowl and stir to combine. Season with salt and set aside.

3. Using a sharp knife, cut the chicken breasts horizontally but don't go all the way through. Stuff the chicken breasts by dividing the mascarpone mixture between the chicken breasts and filling the 'pocket' you have created. Secure with one or two cocktail sticks.

4. Put the filled chicken into a medium roasting dish and season with salt and pepper. Pour the stock around the chicken and roast in the oven for 25 minutes or until cooked through.

5. Remove the cocktail sticks and serve with some boiled new potatoes.

GINO'S TIP: You can use mint sauce if you don't have any fresh mint and for a lighter filling use ricotta instead of mascarpone.

Per serving	Kcal	Fat	Saturates	Carbs	Sugars	Fibre	Protein	Salt
	317	14g	8g	2g	1g	0.1g	47g	0.5g

GAMMON STEAKS WITH BROAD BEANS AND WHITE WINE

Gammon and ham are both cuts taken from the hind leg of a pig. So what's the difference? Well, ham is the meat in its cooked or cured form and is ready to eat, whereas gammon is raw, ready to be cooked by you. These steaks make a really speedy and delicious family supper – on the table in minutes.

SERVES 4

400g frozen broad beans
1 tablespoon olive oil
50g unsalted butter
4 gammon steaks, about
    150g each
1 onion, peeled and finely
    chopped
1 garlic clove, peeled and
    finely chopped
1 bay leaf
1 teaspoon dried oregano
100ml white wine
100ml hot low-salt chicken
    stock
3 tablespoons fresh flat-leaf
    parsley, chopped
Freshly ground black pepper

1. Preheat the oven to 100°C/gas mark ½.

2. Bring a small saucepan of water to the boil and drop in the broad beans. Boil for 3 minutes. Drain and refresh under cold running water, then set aside.

2. Put the olive oil and half the butter into a large 30cm frying pan and place over a high heat. When the butter starts to foam, add the gammon steaks and fry for 3 minutes on each side. Season with pepper – you won't need salt as the gammon is already salty.

3. Remove the gammon from the pan, transfer to a baking tray and place in the oven to keep warm while you prepare the rest of the dish.

4. Add the remaining butter to the same frying pan you cooked the gammon in and place over a medium heat. Add in the onion and fry for 3 minutes, stirring occasionally with a wooden spoon. Add the garlic, bay leaf and oregano and cook for a further 2 minutes. Add the wine and let it bubble for 1 minute to cook off the alcohol.

5. Add the chicken stock and the broad beans. Bring to the boil and continue to cook for 2 minutes. Stir in the parsley.

6. Remove the gammon from the oven, transfer to serving plates and spoon over the broad beans and sauce. Season with black pepper and serve immediately.

GINO'S TIP: To stop gammon steaks curling up as you cook them, just snip the fat around the edge at intervals of a few centimetres.

Per serving	Kcal	Fat	Saturates	Carbs	Sugars	Fibre	Protein	Salt
	456	24g	10g	15g	4g	10g	37g	3.46g

ROASTED CHICKEN LEGS WITH THYME AND CHICKPEAS

This is another great dish for an autumn weekend lunch or dinner. Chicken legs have more flavour than chicken breasts, but they do take longer to cook – so they're perfect for slow cooking. This one-pot dish just cooks away happily while you get on with other things; it needs only a few interventions. It's a really satisfying main course that needs just a little brown rice or just a simple green salad served alongside it.

SERVES 4

4 chicken legs
1 large red onion, peeled and sliced
1 teaspoon garlic salt
1 teaspoon fresh thyme leaves
100ml hot chicken stock
3 tablespoons olive oil
2 parsnips, peeled and cut into quarters lengthways
300g butternut squash, peeled and cut into 2cm chunks
1 x 400g tin of chickpeas, drained
1 x 400g tin of chopped tomatoes
Salt and freshly ground black pepper

1. Preheat the oven to 200°C/gas mark 6.

2. Put the chicken legs into a large roasting tray measuring about 25 x 30cm. Add the onion, garlic salt, thyme and chicken stock and drizzle over 2 of the tablespoons of oil. Roast in the oven for 20 minutes.

3. Put the parsnips and butternut squash into a medium bowl and drizzle over the remaining oil. Stir to combine. Remove the chicken from the oven and add the parsnips and butternut squash to the roasting tray. Season with salt and pepper and return to the oven for a further 30 minutes.

4. Remove the chicken from the oven and scatter over the chickpeas and tomatoes. Give it a good stir and return to the oven for a final 35 minutes.

5. Serve hot with boiled brown rice.

GINO'S TIP: Use chicken legs with the bone in – they're not only cheaper, but also have much more flavour.

Per serving	Kcal	Fat	Saturates	Carbs	Sugars	Fibre	Protein	Salt
	481	25g	5g	31g	14g	11g	26g	1.1g

THE ULTIMATE SIMPLE MEATLOAF

Meatloaf is basically one giant meatball and makes a delicious and economical meal to serve the whole family. It is so simple; you just need to combine all the ingredients, roll them in polenta flour to get a lovely crunchy coating, then leave it to bake slowly until juicy, tender and flavoursome. It's delicious served hot with mashed potatoes and some green veg, or cold in slices on a picnic or for a packed lunch.

SERVES 4

3 slices of white bread, crust removed
500ml cold water
600g beef mince
2 red onions, peeled and finely chopped
1 large carrot, peeled and grated
2 teaspoons dried oregano
100ml hot beef stock
2 eggs, lightly beaten
30g polenta flour
Salt and freshly ground black pepper

1. Break the bread into small pieces and put into a small bowl. Pour over 500ml cold water and leave to soak for 15 minutes. Meanwhile, preheat the oven to 180°C/gas mark 4.

2. Put the meat into a large bowl and add the onions, carrot and oregano. Squeeze the water from the bread until it stops dripping. Add the bread to the meat and discard the water. Using your hands, mix all the ingredients together to combine.

3. Add the beef stock and eggs and season with salt and pepper. Mix thoroughly to combine.

4. Sprinkle the polenta flour onto a chopping board. Shape the beef into a loaf measuring about 25 x 12cm and then roll in the polenta. Transfer the loaf to a large roasting tray and place in the oven for 1¼ hours until browned and the juices run clear.

5. Serve with creamy mashed potato and green vegetables.

GINO'S TIP: Make sure the beef mince you use here is not too lean, otherwise the meatloaf will dry out during roasting – you want something that is at least 10% fat.

Per serving	Kcal	Fat	Saturates	Carbs	Sugars	Fibre	Protein	Salt
	482	27g	11g	20g	6g	3g	36g	0.68g

CRISPY TOPPED CHICKEN BREAST WITH TOMATOES AND BASIL

Chicken is a great source of lean protein, so this simple dish will keep you feeling fuller for longer. It's ideal for feeding a family – it's got a little heat from the chilli, but it's not overpowering for young palates. We cook chicken a lot in my house, so we are always trying to find ways to make it more interesting. This is one of my solutions – simple and delicious. It's great any time of year and just needs a big salad with it – or, on a cold day, perhaps some lightly steamed green beans.

SERVES 4

4 skinless chicken breasts
1 x 400g tin of chopped tomatoes, drained of some of their liquid
1 tablespoon tomato purée
10 basil leaves, sliced
2 slices of white bread, blitzed into breadcrumbs in a food processor
1 teaspoon chilli powder
2 tablespoons extra virgin olive oil
Salt and freshly ground black pepper

1. Preheat the oven to 180°C/gas mark 4.

2. Cut each chicken breast horizontally so you have 2 thin breasts per portion, then put the chicken breasts into a large roasting tray measuring about 25 x 30cm. Season with salt and pepper and set aside.

3. Pour the tomatoes into a small bowl, add the tomato purée and basil and stir together. Put the breadcrumbs into a small bowl and stir in the chilli powder and oil. Set aside.

4. Evenly spread the tomatoes over the chicken and then sprinkle over the breadcrumbs. Bake in the oven for 25 minutes or until the top is golden and crispy and the chicken is thoroughly cooked through.

5. Serve with a big mixed salad or some steamed vegetables.

Per serving	Kcal	Fat	Saturates	Carbs	Sugars	Fibre	Protein	Salt
	276	10g	2g	10g	4g	2g	36g	0.38g

SWEET MARINATED LAMB CHOPS WITH FRESH ROSEMARY

Lamb is traditionally eaten at Easter and no family table at that time of year would be without it. There is nothing nicer than perfectly cooked lamb, just slightly pink; like many Italians, I love it served with a sweet sauce. The lamb chops are marinated in the traditional accompaniments here – redcurrant jelly and fresh rosemary – and the longer you leave them, the better the flavour. But hey, you don't have to save this for Easter – it's *fantastico* any time!

SERVES 4

1 x 340g jar redcurrant jelly
100ml chicken stock, at room temperature
2 tablespoons fresh rosemary leaves, finely chopped
1 tablespoon balsamic vinegar
1 teaspoon garlic salt
8 lamb chops

1. Put the redcurrant jelly, chicken stock, rosemary, balsamic vinegar and garlic salt into a small bowl. Stir to combine.

2. Lay the chops, in a single layer, in a ceramic dish. Pour over the marinade, cover with cling film and place in the fridge to marinate for at least 4 hours.

3. When you are ready to cook, preheat the grill to high.

4. Remove the chops from the ceramic dish and put onto a baking tray, reserving the marinade. Place the chops under the grill for 6 minutes, turning halfway through.

5. Meanwhile, pour the marinade into a small saucepan and bring to the boil. Reduce the heat to very low and leave to bubble while the chops cook.

6. Serve the chops with the marinade drizzled over and a few boiled new potatoes on the side.

GINO'S TIP: Take your lamb chops out of the fridge at least 30 minutes before cooking so that they can come up to room temperature.

Per serving	Kcal 526	Fat 17g	Saturates 7g	Carbs 53g	Sugars 52g	Fibre 0.4g	Protein 41g	Salt 1.2g

SPICY CHILLI CHICKEN

This is another great dish that works beautifully in either summer or winter. This light sauce is a good source of vitamin C and combines amazingly with the chicken to make a really comforting supper after a long cold day. But don't save it for winter; the chilli sauce makes a terrific marinade for barbecuing the chicken on a summer's day.

SERVES 4

2 red chillies, deseeded and roughly chopped

1 red pepper, deseeded and roughly chopped

15g flat-leaf parsley

3 tablespoons red wine vinegar

3 tablespoons extra virgin olive oil

½ teaspoon salt

4 skinless chicken breasts

1. Put the chillies, red pepper, parsley, vinegar, extra virgin olive oil and salt into a food processor and whizz until combined. Don't over process as you want some texture.

2. Make 3 diagonal slashes across the top of each chicken breast. Put them into a roasting dish measuring about 25 x 30cm and pour two-thirds of the chilli sauce over the top. Try and cover as much of the surface of the chicken as you can. Cover with cling film and transfer to the fridge to marinate for about 4 hours.

3. Remove the chicken from the fridge and leave it to rest at room temperature for 15 minutes.

4. Place a 25cm griddle pan over a medium heat. Add the chicken breasts and cook for about 8 minutes on each side.

5. Serve hot with plain boiled rice and the remaining chilli sauce drizzled over.

GINO'S TIP: This is a great get-ahead recipe; if you like, you can marinate the chicken the day before and leave the flavours to infuse overnight.

Per serving	Kcal	Fat	Saturates	Carbs	Sugars	Fibre	Protein	Salt
	287	13g	2g	2g	2g	1g	40g	0.8g

PORK BELLY WITH SPINACH, WATERCRESS AND HAZELNUTS

This classic Piedmontese recipe uses pork belly, which is a pretty cheap cut that needs slow-roasting to get the best from it. It's well worth the wait, though! For the perfect pork belly, make sure the oven is hot when you first add the meat and do follow this recipe carefully, adjusting the oven temperatures as instructed. This ensures you get the perfect combination of tender flesh and crisp crackling. The pepperiness of the rocket and watercress are perfect with the rich meat and the hazelnuts add extra crunch.

SERVES 4

500g pork belly, cut into
   4 strips
1 red onion, peeled and cut
   into 4 slices
1 tablespoon vegetable oil
500ml boiling water
80g blanched hazelnuts
80g mixed bag of fresh
   spinach, rocket and
   watercress
1 tablespoon red wine
   vinegar
Salt and freshly ground black
   pepper

1. Preheat the oven to 220°C/gas mark 7.

2. Using a very sharp knife, score the skin of the pork with several slits. Put the onion slices into a roasting tin and sit the pork on top with the skin facing upwards. Brush the skin with the oil, season well with salt and roast in the oven for 30 minutes.

3. Reduce the oven temperature to 160°/gas mark 3. Pour the water around the onions and continue to cook for 1 hour.

4. Remove the roasting tin from the oven and rest at room temperature for 15 minutes.

5. Meanwhile, increase the oven temperature to 180°C/gas mark 4, tip the hazelnuts onto a baking tray and toast for 8 minutes or until slightly browned. Remove from the oven and leave to cool. Roughly chop them and set aside.

6. Arrange the spinach, rocket and watercress salad onto a large serving platter. Scatter over the nuts and drizzle over 4 tablespoons of the cooking liquid and the vinegar.

7. Arrange the pork on top of the leaves, season with salt and pepper and serve immediately.

Per serving	Kcal	Fat	Saturates	Carbs	Sugars	Fibre	Protein	Salt
	414	33g	7g	4g	3g	2g	24g	0.2g

BRAISED CHICKEN THIGHS WITH CANNELLINI BEANS

This is a great one-pot dish, creamy and comforting, hearty and yet not high in fat. Beans are widely used in Italian dishes as a healthy alternative to meat, or to inexpensively bulk out a meat dish. They are so good for you; they provide protein and soluble fibre, making this a really satisfying meal in one.

SERVES 4

2 tablespoons olive oil
8 chicken thighs, skin removed
2 onions, peeled and roughly chopped
2 garlic cloves, peeled and crushed
1 tablespoon fresh rosemary leaves, finely chopped
50ml white wine
500ml hot chicken stock (made with stock cubes)

1. Pour the oil into a large lidded wide saucepan and place over a medium heat. Add the chicken and brown for 6 minutes, turning halfway through. Add the onions, garlic and rosemary and cook for a further 2 minutes, stirring occasionally with a wooden spoon.

2. Pour in the wine and let it bubble for 1 minute to cook off the alcohol.

3. Scrape the bottom of the pan to incorporate all the brown bits. Pour in the stock with the tomato purée and bring to the boil. Season with salt and pepper, then reduce the heat to a simmer and leave to cook for 25 minutes with the lid off, followed by 20 minutes with the lid on.

1 tablespoon tomato purée
2 x 400g tins of cannellini
  beans, drained
50g reduced-fat mascarpone
  cheese
10g fresh flat-leaf parsley,
  finely chopped
Salt and freshly ground black
  pepper

4. Add the cannellini beans and mascarpone cheese and stir to combine. Continue to cook for a further 10 minutes.

5. Scatter over the parsley and serve hot.

Per serving	Kcal 536	Fat 26g	Saturates 7g	Carbs 21g	Sugars 6g	Fibre 9g	Protein 48g	Salt 2.3g

CHICKEN AND PEPPER SKEWERS

Skewered meat recipes are great when you want (as you should!) to get the kids involved – even the littlest hands can help you thread the chicken or peppers. Low in fat, light and colourful, these are fabulous on the barbecue in summer, but also excellent as a speedy midweek supper at any other time of the year. If your weekdays are busy, prepare the chicken in the morning and leave it marinating in the fridge all day.

SERVES 4

150ml low-fat natural yogurt
2 tablespoons olive oil
2 garlic cloves, peeled and crushed
1 teaspoon smoked paprika
30g fresh flat-leaf parsley, roughly chopped
8 skinless and boneless chicken thighs, cut into chunks
1 onion, peeled and cut into chunks
½ red pepper, deseeded and cut into chunks
½ yellow pepper, deseeded and cut into chunks
Salt and freshly ground black pepper

1. Pour the yogurt into a medium bowl. Add the olive oil, garlic, paprika and parsley. Season with salt and pepper and stir to combine. Add the chicken pieces and stir to coat. Cover with cling film and transfer to the fridge to marinate for 2 hours.

2. When you are ready to cook, preheat the grill to high.

3. Remove the chicken from the fridge and thread onto wooden skewers, alternating the red and yellow peppers and onions.

4. Put the skewers onto a baking tray and cook under the hot grill for 20 minutes, turning halfway through, until the chicken is golden brown and slightly charred.

5. Serve with your favourite salad.

GINO'S TIP: When using wooden skewers soak them in water for a few minutes beforehand – this prevents them from burning. This is a fantastic recipe to make on a barbecue in the summer.

Per serving	Kcal	Fat	Saturates	Carbs	Sugars	Fibre	Protein	Salt
	280	16g	4g	8g	7g	3g	25g	0.3g

CHICKEN BREASTS IN CREAMY SAGE AND LIME SAUCE

Chicken breasts are such a great option for an easy, quick and healthy midweek supper and this creamy sauce has a fabulous citrusy kick. I like to serve this with a simple crisp green salad and some boiled new potatoes or – even better – my Mushroom Rice.

SERVES 4

50g salted butter, at room temperature
2 limes
4 skinless chicken breasts
10g fresh sage, finely chopped
4 tablespoons hot chicken stock
100g reduced-fat mascarpone cheese
Salt and freshly ground black pepper

For the mushroom rice
15g salted butter
150g closed cup mushrooms, thinly sliced
1 spring onion, finely chopped
450ml hot chicken stock
200g long-grain rice (white or brown)
3 tablespoons fresh flat-leaf parsley, finely chopped

1. Preheat the oven to 200°C/gas mark 6.

2. Put the butter into a small bowl with the grated zest of 1 of the limes and mix until combined. Set aside.

3. Using a sharp knife, score each chicken breast with 3 or 4 deep diagonal cuts. Transfer the chicken to a flameproof roasting tray and dot with the lime butter. Squeeze the juice from both limes and pour over the chicken. Sprinkle over the sage and season with salt and pepper. Roast in the oven for 25 minutes.

4. Meanwhile, prepare the rice. Put the butter into a medium saucepan and fry the mushrooms and spring onions over a medium heat for 5 minutes, stirring occasionally with a wooden spoon.

5. Pour in the stock and then add the rice together with the parsley. Bring to the boil, cover with a lid and reduce the heat to low. Cook for 20 minutes or until the rice has absorbed all the liquid. Stir occasionally with a wooden spoon and, once ready, season with salt and pepper.

6. Transfer the cooked chicken onto warm serving plates and cover to keep warm while you make the sauce.

7. Place the roasting tray in which you cooked the chicken over a medium heat and pour in a tablespoon of the chicken stock. Scrape the bottom of the tray to remove any brown bits and bring to the boil. Reduce the heat and stir in the mascarpone cheese. Add the remaining stock to loosen the sauce, stir all together and check the seasoning.

8. Pour the sauce over the chicken breasts and serve with the delicious mushroom rice.

GINO'S TIP: To get maximum juice from limes, make sure they are at room temperature and roll them gently between your palms before squeezing them.

Per serving	Kcal	Fat	Saturates	Carbs	Sugars	Fibre	Protein	Salt
	593	24g	14g	42g	1g	2g	51g	0.9g

LEMON CHICKEN WITH HONEY AND ROSEMARY

Rosemary and lemon give this simple chicken dish a real taste of the Mediterranean; it is zingy and flavoursome but really child-friendly, so it makes a great midweek family meal. Perfect in summer with a big salad, or try it in winter for a serious vitamin C kick to beat the bugs.

SERVES 4

3 lemons
25g salted butter
2 tablespoons runny honey
1 garlic clove, peeled and crushed
2 tablespoons fresh rosemary leaves
8 chicken drumsticks
2 large potatoes, peeled and cut into 2cm chunks
Salt and freshly ground black pepper

1. Preheat the oven to 190°C/gas mark 5.

2. Squeeze the juice from 2 of the lemons and pour into a small saucepan. Add the butter, honey, garlic and rosemary. Place over a low heat for 2 minutes, stirring occasionally; set aside.

3. Arrange the chicken drumsticks in a large roasting tray. Scatter the potatoes around the chicken and pour over the hot lemon sauce. Cut the remaining lemon into 4 and place in the tray. Stir to ensure that the sauce is coating all the chicken and potatoes and everything is evenly spaced. Season with salt and pepper and roast in the oven for 1¼ hours, stirring halfway through.

4. Remove from the oven and serve with a big mixed salad.

GINO'S TIP: The lemon and honey make a great sauce for roasting, but you could also use it as a marinade for barbecuing chicken in summer.

Per serving	Kcal	Fat	Saturates	Carbs	Sugars	Fibre	Protein	Salt
	358	14g	6g	30g	9g	3g	27g	0.43g

BAKED MEATBALLS IN SPICY TOMATO SAUCE

Meatballs are a real family favourite and a midweek supper staple in my house, but I like to give them a grown-up twist with a good punch of chilli every now and again. Baking the meatballs instead of frying them is much easier and less messy – they don't fall apart from constant turning and you don't need to stand over them while they cook. They are healthier, too, because you don't need as much oil.

SERVES 4

500g beef mince
1 onion, peeled and grated
1 slice of white bread, blitzed into breadcrumbs in a food processor
15g fresh flat-leaf parsley, finely chopped
1 teaspoon dried oregano
1 teaspoon garlic salt
1 red chilli, deseeded and finely chopped
1 egg, lightly beaten
2 tablespoons vegetable oil
2 x 400g tins of chopped tomatoes
1 teaspoon caster sugar
Salt and freshly ground black pepper

1. Preheat the oven to 200°C/gas mark 6.

2. Put the beef, onion, breadcrumbs, parsley, oregano, garlic salt, half the chilli and egg into a large bowl. Mix until just combined then, using dampened hands, take small amounts of the mixture and roll into balls about the size of a golf ball. You should get about 20 meatballs. Place them in a roasting tray measuring about 25 x 30cm in a single layer. Drizzle with the oil and bake in the oven for 15 minutes.

3. Meanwhile, put the tinned tomatoes, sugar and remaining chilli into a medium saucepan over a medium heat. Season with salt and simmer gently until the meatballs have had their time in the oven.

4. Remove the meatballs from the oven and tip into the pan with the tomatoes. Bring to the boil, reduce the heat to a simmer and continue to cook for a further 25 minutes.

5. Season with black pepper and serve immediately with rice.

GINO'S TIP: If you prefer a less rich meatball, you can use half pork and half beef mince.

Per serving	Kcal	Fat	Saturates	Carbs	Sugars	Fibre	Protein	Salt
	427	27g	9g	14g	11g	3g	30g	1.6g

MEAT-FREE

Meat-free Monday is gaining quite a following in this country – it's a good idea for both your health and your wallet. In Italy we have such an abundance of fresh vegetables that when I'm there I don't miss meat too much. These recipes will prove to you that with a rainbow of veg you can create delicious dishes. The meals won't leave you feeling hungry either, especially with the addition of protein-rich eggs and cheese.

SPICY BAKED AUBERGINES WITH PARMESAN CHEESE

No Italian cookery book is complete without this classic Northern Italian dish and nearly every chef has his or her own version. Mine has the obligatory chilli to give it some heat, offset by creamy ricotta and mozzarella. Aubergines are packed with vitamins, minerals and dietary fibre and can also lower cholesterol, so this is a really healthy as well as hearty bake. If there's any left over, it's great cold the next day too.

SERVES 4

2 tablespoons olive oil, plus extra for brushing
3 medium aubergines
Juice of 1 lemon
1 onion, peeled and roughly chopped
2 x 400g tins of chopped tomatoes
1 teaspoon dried chilli flakes
1 teaspoon dried oregano
100g ricotta cheese
100g mozzarella cheese, cut into small pieces
2 large round tomatoes, thinly sliced
25g freshly grated Parmesan cheese
Salt and freshly ground black pepper

1. Preheat the oven to 190°C/gas mark 5 and brush 3 large baking trays with a little oil.

2. Trim and discard the bottom and top of the aubergines. Cut each aubergine into slices about 5mm thick and lay the slices onto the baking trays.

3. Pour 1 tablespoon of olive oil into a small bowl and stir in the lemon juice. Brush the aubergines with half of the oil and lemon juice mixture. Season and bake in the oven for 15 minutes. Remove from the oven and turn the slices over. Brush with the remaining oil and lemon juice and return to the oven for a further 15 minutes. Set aside.

4. Pour the remaining oil into a medium saucepan and place over a medium heat. Fry the onion for 5 minutes, stirring occasionally. Add the tinned tomatoes, chilli and oregano and gently cook for 25 minutes, stirring occasionally. Remove from the heat and blitz with a hand-held blender until smooth. Add salt and set aside.

5. Spread 2 tablespoons of the tomato sauce over the bottom of an ovenproof dish measuring about 25 x 20cm. Lay over a third of the aubergine slices. Spread over a third of the tomato sauce. Dot over half of the ricotta, and half the mozzarella cheese. Season with salt and pepper. Repeat with another third of the aubergines, a third of the tomato sauce, and the remaining ricotta and mozzarella. Finish with the remaining aubergines, the sliced tomatoes and remaining tomato sauce.

6. Sprinkle over the Parmesan cheese, season with pepper and bake in the oven for 25 minutes. Serve hot or at room temperature.

GINO'S TIP: Aubergine flesh can turn brown really quickly once cut, so slice your aubergines only when you are ready to cook them. Aubergines will soak up the oil like a sponge: to lessen the problem, sprinkle salt over the slices and leave in a colander for 30 minutes, then rise with water and pat dry.

Per serving	Kcal	Fat	Saturates	Carbs	Sugars	Fibre	Protein	Salt
	318	17g	8g	20g	19g	15g	12g	0.5g

STUFFED RED PEPPERS WITH BASIL PESTO AND TALEGGIO CHEESE

I love this recipe; it's so easy to prepare and looks fantastic, with all the colours of the Italian flag! Peppers soften beautifully on cooking, releasing delicious juices that stop the stuffing drying out in the oven. Taleggio is a gorgeous, mellow, Northern Italian cheese that oozes decadently when melted, adding a creamy texture. This is a brilliant family supper that's on the table in half an hour.

SERVES 4

4 red peppers, tops sliced off and core and seeds removed
2 tablespoons olive oil
150g couscous
2 tablespoons ready-made basil pesto
130ml hot vegetable stock
100g Taleggio cheese, cut into small pieces
100g pitted green olives in brine, drained and roughly chopped
1 slice of white bread, blitzed into breadcrumbs in a food processor
Salt and freshly ground black pepper

1. Preheat the oven to 200°C/gas mark 6.

2. Brush the peppers with the oil and sit them upright in a muffin tin. Season with salt and pepper and bake in the oven for 10 minutes.

3. Meanwhile, put the couscous into a medium bowl, add the pesto and hot vegetable stock and stir to mix. Cover with cling film and leave for 5 minutes to allow the couscous to absorb the liquid. Remove the cling film and fluff the couscous up using a fork.

4. Add the Taleggio and green olives to the couscous. Stir all together and then use the mixture to fill the peppers. Sprinkle over the breadcrumbs and season with salt and pepper.

5. Bake in the oven for 20 minutes. Serve hot with a beautiful cherry tomato salad dressed with extra virgin olive oil and balsamic glaze.

GINO'S TIP: The couscous stuffing also makes a delicious salad for the lunchbox – so if you have too much to stuff into your peppers, put it in the fridge for the next day.

Per serving	Kcal	Fat	Saturates	Carbs	Sugars	Fibre	Protein	Salt
	384	19g	6g	38g	8g	6g	12g	1.8g

SOUFFLÉ OMELETTE WITH ARTICHOKES AND ROASTED PEPPERS

For those of you who don't like the texture of a traditional frittata, prepare to be seduced by this delicious variation. A final touch under the grill puffs up the egg whites to create a beautifully light omelette. This is a really good mix of traditional Italian ingredients and, when combined with a fresh tomato and onion salad, will set you well on your way towards that magic 5 a day.

SERVES 4

8 large eggs
100g tinned artichoke hearts in brine, drained and roughly chopped
100g roasted peppers in oil, drained and roughly chopped
50g pitted green olives in brine, drained and roughly chopped
50g freshly grated Pecorino cheese
15 basil leaves, finely shredded
10g salted butter
2 tablespoons olive oil
Salt and freshly ground black pepper

1. Put 2 whole eggs and 6 egg yolks into a medium bowl. Using a hand-held electric whisk, beat until all combined and set aside. Clean the whisk beaters.

2. Put the remaining 6 egg whites into a separate medium bowl. Using a hand-held electric whisk, beat the egg whites until stiff.

3. Use a large metal spoon to carefully fold the egg whites into the yolks, keeping in as much air as possible. Gently fold in the artichokes, peppers, olives, half the Pecorino cheese and the basil. Season with salt and pepper.

4. Preheat the grill to high.

5. Melt the butter with the oil in a medium (24cm) non-stick frying pan over a medium heat. Pour in the omelette mixture, making sure that it is evenly spread in the pan. Cook for about 6 minutes or until the underneath is golden. Sprinkle over the remaining Pecorino cheese. Transfer the pan to the grill and continue to cook for a further 2 minutes until golden.

6. Run a knife around the edge of the omelette to loosen and slide onto a serving plate. Let it rest for 1 minute. Cut into wedges and serve with a tomato and red onion salad.

GINO'S TIP: Watch your frittata carefully – don't be tempted to overbake it to make sure the egg is cooked. It will make the texture rubbery.

Per serving	Kcal	Fat	Saturates	Carbs	Sugars	Fibre	Protein	Salt
	337	25g	8g	5g	1g	1g	22g	1.8g

COUSCOUS SALAD WITH OLIVES, ASPARAGUS AND GRANA PADANO

Couscous is so easy to prepare, but it does need the addition of some really good flavours to make it come to life. This rainbow salad is a fantastic source of vitamin C and is surprisingly filling. It's great as a main course or you can reduce the quantities and serve it as a side with barbecued meats or grilled fish.

SERVES 4

350ml vegetable stock
250g couscous
100g asparagus tips
1 yellow pepper, deseeded and cut into thin strips
10 cherry tomatoes, cut into quarters
50g pitted black olives in brine, drained and roughly chopped
50g Grana Padano cheese, coarsely grated
4 tablespoons fresh chives, chopped

For the dressing
6 tablespoons extra virgin olive oil
2 tablespoons red wine vinegar
1 teaspoon English mustard
Salt and freshly ground black pepper

1. Pour the vegetable stock into a medium lidded saucepan and bring to the boil. Add the couscous and stir. Cover, reduce the heat and simmer for 5 minutes or until all the water has been absorbed. Remove from the heat and leave to stand with the lid on for 10 minutes. Uncover and fluff the couscous up with a fork, then set aside to cool.

2. Meanwhile, bring a medium saucepan of salted water to the boil. Drop in the asparagus and cook for 3 minutes. Drain and drop into cold water to refresh them – this keeps them crunchy and retains their beautiful green colour. Drain and chop into 2cm pieces and put into a large bowl.

3. Add the pepper, tomatoes, olives, Grana Padano and chives to the asparagus. Set aside.

4. To make the dressing, pour the extra virgin olive oil, vinegar and mustard into a small bowl. Season with salt and pepper and whisk to combine. Pour the dressing into the bowl over the vegetables.

5. Add the cooled couscous and stir all together. Serve on a large platter with a few cold beers.

Per serving	Kcal	Fat	Saturates	Carbs	Sugars	Fibre	Protein	Salt
	502	25g	5g	53g	6g	6g	15g	0.8g

BAKED POTATOES WITH BROCCOLI AND OOZING GORGONZOLA CHEESE

The baked potato is the classic midweek supper staple – so easy to chuck in the oven to provide a filling, satisfying meal at the end of a long day. My kids love baked potatoes, but we need to change up the toppings every now and then to keep them interested. Broccoli and Gorgonzola make a great combination in soups and other dishes, so I thought why not try it on a potato? The result? *Delizioso!*

SERVES 4

4 large baking potatoes
25g salted butter
200g broccoli, cut into small
 florets
80g closed cup mushrooms,
 sliced
100g Gorgonzola cheese
8 medium eggs
Salt and freshly ground black
 pepper

1. Preheat the oven to 180°C/gas mark 4.

2. Bake the potatoes directly on the shelf of the oven for 1½ hours or until they are cooked through and the skins are crispy.

3. Melt the butter in a medium saucepan over a medium heat. Add the broccoli with the mushrooms, season with salt and pepper and fry for 8 minutes, stirring occasionally with a wooden spoon. Set aside.

4. Remove the potatoes from the oven and cut each potato in half lengthways. Using a tablespoon, gently scoop out the insides, keeping the skins intact. Put the potato flesh into a medium bowl, season with salt and pepper and mash. Stir the broccoli and mushrooms into the potato.

5. Use the mixture to fill the cavity of the reserved potato skins, then place on baking tray. Cut the Gorgonzola into 24 little pieces and poke 3 pieces of the Gorgonzola into each potato half.

6. Using the back of a teaspoon, make a well in the middle of each potato. Carefully crack an egg into each well. Return to the oven for 15 minutes or until the eggs have just set.

7. Serve with a beautiful tomato salad dressed with olive oil and balsamic vinegar.

Per serving	Kcal	Fat	Saturates	Carbs	Sugars	Fibre	Protein	Salt
	524	23g	11g	49g	4g	8g	27g	1.33g

STUFFED BAKED AUBERGINES WITH THYME AND MOZZARELLA

Peppers are usually the obvious vegetable to be stuffed, but aubergines make an interesting variation. Aubergine, tomatoes and mozzarella are a match made in heaven, but here I've added fennel for a mild aniseed kick. This needs a little prep, but it's so worth it. It's a really substantial meal, needing only a simple salad alongside it.

SERVES 4

2 large aubergines, sliced in half lengthways
2 tablespoons olive oil
1 red onion, peeled and finely chopped
½ fennel bulb, cored and thinly sliced
250g tinned chopped tomatoes
2 tablespoons tomato purée
1 teaspoon fresh thyme leaves
1 x 125g mozzarella ball, drained and cut into small cubes
Salt and freshly ground black pepper

1. Preheat the oven to 180°C/gas mark 4.

2. Score the flesh of the aubergine with a criss-cross pattern and put onto a baking tray, skin side down. Bake in the oven for 25 minutes.

3. Meanwhile, pour the oil into a medium saucepan, add the onion and fry over a medium heat for 5 minutes, stirring occasionally with a wooden spoon. Add the fennel and continue to cook for 2 minutes, stirring. Add the tomatoes, tomato purée, thyme leaves and season with salt and pepper. Continue to cook for a further 10 minutes, stirring occasionally.

4. Remove the aubergines from the oven and, using a tablespoon, gently scoop out the flesh, keeping the skin intact. Put the flesh on a chopping board and roughly chop, then add to the tomato sauce and mix.

5. Use the tomato mixture to fill the cavity in the reserved aubergine skins, then return to the baking tray. Dot the mozzarella evenly over the top of the aubergines and return to the oven for 10 minutes.

6. Remove from the oven, sprinkle over some black pepper and serve hot with a simple mixed salad.

Per serving	Kcal	Fat	Saturates	Carbs	Sugars	Fibre	Protein	Salt
	237	13g	5g	13g	12g	11g	10g	0.4g

POLENTA WITH MARINATED GRIDDLED VEGETABLES

Polenta, made of maize flour, was traditionally known as a poor man's food; no self-respecting chef or restaurant would serve it on their menu. But polenta is an amazingly versatile ingredient, as well as being cheap, so has fought its way back onto the dinner table. It can be served as an alternative to mash, used to add a crunchy coating to chicken, fish or my Ultimate Simple Meatloaf (see page 123), or it can even be used in baking as a gluten-free additive. Polenta needs some strong flavours around it to make it interesting, so it works really well with a variety of roast veg.

SERVES 4

750ml vegetable stock
175g quick-cook polenta
25g salted butter
3 tablespoons fresh flat-leaf parsley, finely chopped
1 fennel bulb, quartered and cored
1 red onion, peeled and cut into 5mm slices
2 large courgettes, halved and each half cut lengthways into 4
2 tomatoes, cut into 5mm slices

For the marinade
4 tablespoons olive oil
2 tablespoons white wine vinegar
1 tablespoon runny honey
2 garlic cloves, peeled and crushed
3 tablespoons fresh flat-leaf parsley, finely chopped
Salt and freshly ground black pepper

1. Pour the vegetable stock into a medium saucepan and bring to the boil. Reduce the heat to low and slowly pour the polenta into the stock, whisking constantly. Continue to cook for 8 minutes, stirring all the time. Remove from the heat and stir in the butter and parsley.

2. Sprinkle a baking tray measuring about 35 x 25cm with cold water. Spread the polenta over the baking tray and set aside to cool while you make the marinade. Pour the olive oil, vinegar and honey into a medium bowl. Stir in the garlic and parsley and season well with salt and pepper.

3. Put the fennel, onion, courgettes and tomatoes into a dish measuring about 25 x 35cm and drizzle over the marinade. Using your hands, turn all the vegetables so that everything is evenly coated. Cover with cling film and transfer to the fridge for 1 hour to marinate.

4. Turn the polenta out onto a flat surface and cut into 12 pieces. Set aside. Remove the vegetables from the fridge. Place a large griddle pan over a high heat and cook the fennel, onion and courgettes for 6 minutes, turning halfway through. Work in batches and arrange the cooked vegetables onto a large serving platter as they are done. Cook the tomato slices for 4 minutes, turning half way through. Again, place the cooked tomatoes onto the serving platter.

5. Add the polenta to the platter. Season and serve with a cold bottle of Vermentino white wine.

Per serving	Kcal	Fat	Saturates	Carbs	Sugars	Fibre	Protein	Salt
	268	17g	5g	20g	12g	6g	5g	1.2g

CHICORY, AVOCADO AND EGG SALAD WITH POPPY SEED DRESSING

Italians love chicory, but the British palate still needs a bit of convincing! It's quite expensive to buy, but again, a little goes a long way in terms of flavour. Chicory comes in all sorts of varieties, including a looser-leafed version and the one with red leaves (radicchio) that has become increasingly familiar as a restaurant salad ingredient. Both have a characteristic bitter taste, but the flavour becomes milder when cooked – and they look and taste amazing when chargrilled or stirred into risottos. In this salad I've used crunchy raw chicory and radishes, both beautifully balanced by creamy avocados, hard-boiled eggs and fresh, juicy tomatoes. It doesn't keep well once dressed, but I doubt you'll have much left once you've served this!

SERVES 4

4 large eggs
1 x 270g pack of chicory, trimmed and leaves separated
½ cucumber, cut lengthways and seeds removed, thinly sliced
100g radishes, thinly sliced
10 yellow cherry tomatoes, cut into quarters
1 large avocado
Juice of 1 lemon

For the dressing
1 tablespoon poppy seeds
4 tablespoons extra virgin olive oil
1 tablespoon white wine vinegar
1 teaspoon runny honey
2 garlic cloves, peeled and crushed
2 teaspoons Dijon mustard
Salt and freshly ground black pepper

1. Put the eggs into a small saucepan and cover with cold water. Bring to the boil, then reduce the heat to a simmer and cook for 7 minutes. Remove from the heat and place the saucepan in the sink. Let the cold water tap continuously run into the saucepan for a couple of minutes or until the eggs are cool enough to handle. Peel the eggs under cold running water and set aside.

2. Arrange the chicory, cucumber, radishes and tomatoes on a large flat serving plate.

3. Cut the avocado into bite-sized chunks and put into a small bowl. Pour over the lemon juice and stir to coat the avocado. Arrange the avocado over the chicory, drizzling over the remaining lemon juice from the bowl.

4. Now make the dressing. Warm a small frying pan over a medium heat and add the poppy seeds. Toast for 3 minutes and leave to cool. Add the seeds to a small mixing bowl together with the oil, vinegar, honey, garlic and Dijon mustard. Whisk to combine and season to taste. Drizzle the dressing over the salad.

5. Halve each egg lengthways and scatter around the serving platter.

6. Enjoy with a cold beer and a few slices of toasted ciabatta bread.

GINO'S TIP: When buying chicory, remember that generally the darker the colour, the more bitter the leaf.

Per serving	Kcal	Fat	Saturates	Carbs	Sugars	Fibre	Protein	Salt
	347	29g	6g	7g	3g	4g	13g	0.6g

SPICY RATATOUILLE WITH EGGS AND PARMESAN CHEESE

This is a great one-pot dish that is perfect for preparing in advance (apart from the eggs, which are added just towards the end of cooking) because the flavours of ratatouille actually improve after a few days in the fridge. I like to bulk out my ratatouille with beans to make it go further. This is a great dish for lunch or dinner or even as brunch the morning after a heavy night. Packed with Vitamin C, folate and fibre, it'll have you back on your feet in no time!

SERVES 4

1 medium aubergine
2 tablespoons olive oil
1 red onion, peeled and
   thinly sliced
1 red pepper, deseeded and
   sliced
10 fresh basil leaves, finely
   chopped
1 teaspoon dried chilli flakes
2 courgettes, halved
   lengthways then cut into
   5mm half-moons
1 x 400g tin of chopped
   tomatoes
1 x 400g tin of borlotti beans,
   drained
50ml hot vegetable stock
4 medium eggs
20g freshly grated Parmesan
   cheese
Salt

1. Slice off and discard the bottom and green top from the aubergine. Cut the aubergine into 1cm cubes and set aside.

2. Pour the oil into a medium lidded casserole and place over a medium heat. Fry the onion for 5 minutes, stirring occasionally with a wooden spoon. Add the pepper and continue to cook for 2 minutes. Add the basil, chilli flakes, aubergine and courgettes and cook for a further 5 minutes, stirring occasionally.

3. Pour in the tomatoes, borlotti beans and vegetable stock. Stir and bring to the boil. Reduce the heat to a simmer and continue to cook for 30 minutes with the lid on and then 10 minutes with the lid off. Stir occasionally and season with salt.

4. Using the back of a spoon make 4 hollows in the ratatouille and crack an egg into each hole. Cover the saucepan with a lid and cook for a further 8 minutes.

5. Carefully ladle into bowls and sprinkle over the Parmesan cheese. Serve immediately.

GINO'S TIP: Ratatouille also freezes really well, so you could double up this recipe and store some for another day.

Per serving	Kcal	Fat	Saturates	Carbs	Sugars	Fibre	Protein	Salt
	299	14g	4g	20g	12g	12g	18g	0.5g

SPINACH AND COURGETTE FRITTATA WITH FRESH MINT

Frittatas are often the go-to recipe for using up leftovers, but I think there are times when it deserves a special recipe all to itself. I'll eat frittata for a light supper, for lunch or even for brunch – and I don't mind whether it's hot or cold. This, for me, is the perfect combination of ingredients – lots of healthy greens with a minty punch and a wonderful creaminess from the melting mozzarella.

SERVES 4

2 tablespoons olive oil

2 red onions, peeled and thinly sliced

1 large courgette, roughly chopped

6 fresh mint leaves, thinly sliced

200g fresh spinach

1 x 125g mozzarella ball, drained and cut into small cubes

8 medium eggs, beaten

Salt and freshly ground black pepper

1. Pour the oil into a large (30cm) non-stick frying pan and place over a medium heat. Add the onions and fry for 6 minutes, stirring occasionally with a wooden spoon. Add the courgette and mint and continue to cook for a further 5 minutes, stirring occasionally.

2. Tip the spinach into a colander and pour over a kettle of boiling water. Cool under cold running water then squeeze as much water out as you can. Scatter the spinach into the frying pan followed by the mozzarella.

3. Preheat the grill to high.

4. Season the eggs with salt and pepper and pour into the frying pan. Using a fork, gently stir so that the eggs are evenly distributed around the vegetables. Cook for 5 minutes until almost completely set.

5. Transfer the frying pan under the grill and continue to cook for a further 3 minutes or until golden brown and cooked through.

6. Serve hot or warm with a simple green salad of your choice.

GINO'S TIP: It's much easier to cut your frittata if you leave it to rest for 5 minutes after cooking.

Per serving	Kcal	Fat	Saturates	Carbs	Sugars	Fibre	Protein	Salt
	321	23g	8g	5g	4g	2g	23g	0.8g

FISH

Fish and seafood play a major part in the Italian diet. I was born and raised on the beautiful Amalfi coast so it's always been a huge part of my life. Fish is another ingredient that can be quite expensive, but you don't need to eat much of it to feel its benefits – and tuna and anchovies can be bought economically in tins. Fish will provide you and your family with a good supply of protein and minerals, particularly the oily types rich in Omega-3, so you should try to eat it at least twice a week.

WRAPPED SALMON WITH DIJON MUSTARD AND MASCARPONE SAUCE

For many people, salmon is the king of fish – it has a firm, meaty texture and a beautiful pink colour. It's really versatile, too – it can be baked, poached, steamed, fried or flaked into stir-fries, pasta or risotto. It's known as a brain food because of its high Omega 3 content, as well as being rich in vitamin D and minerals. This is a delicious way to get all the family eating fish – creamy, comforting and delicious.

SERVES 4

1 courgette, trimmed
400g skinless salmon fillet, cut into 4 pieces
40g salted butter
100ml hot vegetable stock
1 teaspoon Dijon mustard
50g reduced-fat mascarpone cheese
1 tablespoon fresh dill, finely chopped
½ teaspoon garlic salt
Salt and freshly ground black pepper

1. Preheat the oven to 200°C/gas mark 6.

2. Using a potato peeler, slice 8 wide ribbons from the courgette lengthways and set aside.

3. Lightly season each salmon fillet with salt and wrap 2 courgette ribbons around each fillet. Transfer the wrapped salmon to a baking tray measuring about 25 x 35cm and evenly dot the butter over. Transfer to the oven and bake for 18 minutes.

4. Dice the remaining courgette and put into a small saucepan. Add the vegetable stock, Dijon mustard, mascarpone cheese, dill and garlic salt and stir all together. Place the saucepan over a low heat and gently cook for 10 minutes, stirring occasionally with a wooden spoon. Make sure that the sauce doesn't boil otherwise it will split.

5. Remove the salmon from the oven and arrange on a serving platter. Pour the mascarpone sauce over and around salmon.

6. Season with black pepper and serve immediately with mashed potatoes.

GINO'S TIP: Bake the salmon parcels seam side down to help prevent the parcels unravelling.

Per serving	Kcal	Fat	Saturates	Carbs	Sugars	Fibre	Protein	Salt
	335	26g	10g	2g	1g	1g	23g	0.9g

ROASTED VEGETABLES WITH PRAWNS AND ROSEMARY

Prawns and roasted vegetables may not spring to mind as an obvious combination, but trust me, this works! I created this during a family holiday on the coast of Sardinia, using fresh prawns and veg. This is a simpler version – there's no messing around with shelling prawns here as you can use the ready-cooked and peeled prawns, which just need heating through in the oven. Prawns are a good source of protein and are low in fat, so when combined with this great selection of vegetables, you have a healthy family one-pot feast.

SERVES 4

500g baby potatoes, cleaned
2 red onions, peeled and cut into wedges
2 courgettes, trimmed and cut into 1cm slices
1 unwaxed lemon, cut into wedges
1 red pepper, deseeded and cut into 2cm chunks
4 tablespoons olive oil
2 large sprigs of rosemary
250g small cooked frozen prawns, defrosted for at least 8 hours in the fridge
Salt and freshly ground black pepper

1. Preheat the oven to 200°C/gas mark 6.

2. Put the potatoes into a small saucepan, cutting any large ones in half. Cover with cold water and bring to the boil. Reduce the heat and simmer for 15 minutes, then drain and tip into a large roasting tray measuring about 25 x 30cm.

3. Add in the onions, courgettes, lemon and red pepper. Pour over the olive oil and use your hands to turn the vegetables over to make sure that they are all evenly coated in the oil. Tuck in the rosemary sprigs, season with salt and pepper and transfer to the oven. Bake for 40 minutes, stirring halfway through.

4. Remove from the oven and scatter over the prawns. Stir to combine, then return to the oven for 10 minutes.

5. Serve immediately with a simple tomato salad dressed with extra virgin olive oil and balsamic vinegar.

GINO'S TIP: Don't forget to remove the woody rosemary stalk from the dish before serving!

Per serving	Kcal	Fat	Saturates	Carbs	Sugars	Fibre	Protein	Salt
	284	12g	2g	26g	8g	6g	15g	1g

BAKED COD WITH CRISPY PARSLEY BREADCRUMBS

Cod can lack a little flavour, but here the crunchy breadcrumb topping, with zesty lemon, capers and herbs, really transforms this familiar fish. I suppose this is a healthy version of the classic breaded fish, baked in the oven rather than fried in lots of oil. It's really easy and you'll feel so virtuous – especially if you use sustainably caught fish, which of course you really should. Even better, it's on the table within 20 minutes.

SERVES 4

2 slices of white bread, blitzed into breadcrumbs in a food processor
2 tablespoons capers in brine, drained and finely chopped
Zest of 1 unwaxed lemon
15g fresh flat-leaf parsley, finely chopped
500g skinless cod fillet, cut into 4 pieces
200g red cherry tomatoes
3 tablespoons extra virgin olive oil
Salt and freshly ground black pepper

1. Preheat the oven to 200°C/gas mark 6.

2. Put the breadcrumbs into a medium bowl and stir in the capers, lemon zest and parsley. Set aside.

3. Lay the cod fillets in a large roasting tray and season with salt and pepper. Divide the breadcrumb mixture equally over the fish, flattening with the back of a tablespoon.

4. Arrange the tomatoes around the fish fillets and season with salt and pepper. Drizzle the oil over the fish and transfer to the oven. Bake for 15 minutes or until the breadcrumb topping is crispy and golden brown.

5. Serve immediately with a simple mixed salad dressed with balsamic vinegar and extra virgin olive oil.

GINO'S TIP: If you can't get hold of sustainably caught cod, you could substitute it with pollock, which will work just as well.

Per serving	Kcal	Fat	Saturates	Carbs	Sugars	Fibre	Protein	Salt
	215	10g	1g	7g	2g	1g	24g	0.7g

HOME-MADE FISH FINGERS IN POLENTA CRUST

When my kids were younger and we were trying to get them to try new foods, these home-made fish fingers were a winner! Low in fat and so easy to make with storecupboard ingredients, they still ask for these when they want something tasty and comforting. They are much cheaper and healthier than the packaged version and if you double up the ingredients, you can make extra and freeze them on a covered baking sheet, ready to whip out of the freezer for a speedy midweek supper.

SERVES 4

450g frozen pollock fillets, defrosted
100g fine polenta
100g dried breadcrumbs
2 tablespoons chives, finely chopped
Zest of 1 unwaxed lemon
1 teaspoon smoked paprika
2 eggs, lightly beaten
2 tablespoons semi-skimmed milk
2 tablespoons olive oil
Salt

1. Preheat the oven to 180°C/gas mark 6 and line a baking tray with non-stick baking parchment.

2. Cut the pollock into 12 fingers and set aside.

3. Put the polenta, breadcrumbs, chives, lemon zest and paprika into a medium bowl. Season with salt and stir to combine. Tip onto a large flat plate and set aside. Crack the eggs into a medium bowl, whisk in the milk and set aside.

4. First roll the fish in the egg mixture and then in the polenta mixture, ensuring all sides are evenly coated. Put onto the lined baking tray and continue until all the fish has been coated with eggs and polenta.

5. Drizzle the oil over the fish fingers and bake in the oven for 10 minutes. Carefully turn the fingers over and continue to cook for a further 10 minutes.

6. Serve with steamed green vegetables or a green salad.

GINO'S TIP: If you are freezing these, lay them out on a baking sheet lined with baking parchment and space out the fingers. Cover with cling film and freeze. Once frozen, they can be transferred to a freezerproof container and won't stick together.

Per serving	Kcal	Fat	Saturates	Carbs	Sugars	Fibre	Protein	Salt
	278	9g	2g	23g	2g	1g	25g	0.9g

MUSSEL AND TOMATO STEW

In Naples, mussels are the seafood that we eat most, mainly because they are a really cheap ingredient on the Amalfi coast, where you'll find them served both as an antipasto and as a *secondo piatto*. This is a really easy dish, which you could serve as a midweek supper for the family or as a starter for six at a dinner party. Traditionally we'd make this with the mussels in their shells, but this version uses defrosted frozen pulled mussels; this removes the worry about checking the shells to see if they are cooked properly, which can put people off cooking them. Garlic bread is a must here!

SERVES 4

400g frozen mussel meat, defrosted in the fridge for a minimum of 8 hours
2 tablespoons olive oil
3 garlic cloves, peeled and finely sliced
150g frozen peas, defrosted
150ml white wine
2 x 400g tins of chopped tomatoes
1 tablespoon tomato purée
3 tablespoons fresh flat-leaf parsley, finely chopped
1 teaspoon dried oregano
Salt and freshly ground black pepper to taste

1. Squeeze out any excess water from the mussels and set aside on kitchen paper to drain.

2. Pour the oil into a large saucepan, add the garlic and place over a medium heat. Fry for 1 minute, then add the peas and continue to fry for 3 minutes, stirring occasionally with a wooden spoon.

3. Pour in the wine, increase the heat to high and let it bubble for 2 minutes. Add the tinned tomatoes, tomato purée, 1 teaspoon of salt and 1 teaspoon of black pepper. Bring to the boil. Reduce the heat and let it simmer for 10 minutes.

4. Stir in the mussels, parsley and oregano. Continue to cook for 5 minutes or until the mussels are thoroughly heated through.

5. Ladle into warm bowls and serve with slices of garlic bread.

GINO'S TIP: Make a double batch and the next day heat through and toss into cooked spaghetti – it makes a beautiful seafood pasta.

Per serving	Kcal	Fat	Saturates	Carbs	Sugars	Fibre	Protein	Salt
	222	8g	1g	13g	11g	4g	17g	0.8g

POLLOCK WITH CAPERS, OLIVES AND FRESH BASIL

Fish Italian-style. All the tastes of the Mediterranean are combined in a delicious and mouth-watering sauce to go with the delicate fish. This is a really versatile sauce that can be used with pasta, grilled chicken or even steak, so I recommend you double the amount and keep it in the fridge for it another night. Make sure the basil is really fresh, to deliver maximum flavour.

SERVES 4

2 tablespoons olive oil
1 red onion, peeled and thinly sliced
100g pitted black olives in brine, drained and cut in half
50g capers in brine, drained
1 x 400g tin of chopped tomatoes
15 basil leaves, roughly sliced
500g frozen pollock, defrosted and cut into 4 pieces
Salt and freshly ground black pepper

1. Pour the oil into a medium frying pan and fry the onion over a medium heat for 5 minutes, stirring occasionally with a wooden spoon.

2. Add the olives and capers to the pan and continue to fry for a further 5 minutes; stir occasionally.

3. Tip in the tomatoes with the basil, season with salt and pepper and continue to cook for 5 minutes, stirring occasionally.

4. Add the pollock fillets, poking them under the cooking liquid. Partially cover the frying pan with a lid and cook for 7 minutes. Remove the lid and gently turn the fish fillets, then continue to cook without the lid for a further 8 minutes.

5. This is fantastic served with steamed green beans.

GINO'S TIP: Go easy on the salt when you season this dish; the capers and olives are quite salty to begin with.

Per serving	Kcal	Fat	Saturates	Carbs	Sugars	Fibre	Protein	Salt
	215	10	1g	7g	2g	1g	24g	0.7g

HONEY GRILLED SALMON WITH BALSAMIC VINEGAR

This is for one of those evenings when you just want a quick dinner so you can spend the evening with your partner. It's a simple yet special salmon recipe with a sweet balsamic and honey marinade that can be prepped in the morning to make the perfect romantic dinner – it only takes minutes to cook and about the same time to clear up, leaving you with time to catch up on other things . . .

SERVES 4

2 tablespoons extra virgin olive oil

1 tablespoon balsamic vinegar

Zest and juice of 1 unwaxed lemon

1 tablespoon runny honey

3 tablespoons fresh flat-leaf parsley, finely chopped

1 garlic clove, peeled and crushed

400g salmon fillet, cut into 4 pieces

Salt and freshly ground black pepper

1. In a small bowl whisk together the extra virgin olive oil, vinegar, lemon zest and juice, honey, parsley and garlic. Season with salt and pepper and set aside.

2. Put the salmon pieces into a shallow bowl and drizzle over the marinade, making sure that all the surfaces of the fish are coated. Cover with cling film and leave to marinate in the fridge for about 1 hour.

3. Preheat the grill to high.

4. Remove the salmon from the marinade and place the fillets onto a foil-lined baking tray (discard the marinade). Cook under the grill for 3 minutes, turn the fillets over and continue to grill for a further 3 minutes. Take care not to overcook the salmon otherwise it will become dry.

5. Serve with boiled new potatoes and a green salad dressed with a little oil and balsamic vinegar.

GINO'S TIP: Salmon is a popular and versatile fish, but it can be expensive to buy. If you can, buy sides of salmon and cut them into fillets yourself, as it is much cheaper. If it is a large piece, you can freeze the cut portions in a sealable freezerproof container.

Per serving	Kcal	Fat	Saturates	Carbs	Sugars	Fibre	Protein	Salt
	287	20g	4g	5g	4g	0.5g	21g	0.1g

SPICY PRAWN CASSEROLE WITH RICE AND WHITE WINE

A great dinner party dish. Prawns and white wine are a perfect pairing, so I've added a splash here and recommend serving the finished dish with a lovely chilled Pinot Grigio for a special meal. It's a casserole made in a non-traditional way, being assembled and cooked together for 15 minutes at the end – so you could also make this with just the prawns and sauce and serve it with pasta.

SERVES 4

200g long-grain white rice
400ml hot vegetable stock
2 tablespoons olive oil
1 large red onion, peeled
  and finely chopped
5 fresh sage leaves, finely
  chopped
1 teaspoon dried chilli flakes
1 bay leaf
100ml white wine
1 x 400g tin of chopped
  tomatoes
170g medium frozen raw
  prawns, defrosted in the
  fridge for at least 8 hours
10 yellow cherry tomatoes
4 tablespoons chives,
  chopped
Salt

1. Preheat the oven to 180°C/gas mark 4.

2. Put the rice into a medium lidded casserole. Pour in the vegetable stock, cover with a lid and place into the oven for 20 minutes.

3. Meanwhile, pour the oil into a medium saucepan and fry the onion over a medium heat for 6 minutes, stirring occasionally with a wooden spoon. Add the sage, chilli, and bay leaf and continue to cook for 1 minute, stirring occasionally. Pour in the wine, increase the heat and bring to the boil. Reduce the heat to medium and let it bubble for 5 minutes. Stir occasionally.

4. Stir in the tinned tomatoes and season with salt. Bring back to the boil then remove from the heat.

5. Remove the casserole from the oven and arrange the prawns on top of the rice, then pour the tomato mixture evenly over the prawns. Cover with the lid and return to the oven for 15 minutes.

6. Just before serving, stir in the cherry tomatoes and chives. Enjoy with a bottle of chilled Pinot Grigio.

ADD 1 GARLIC CLOVE

Per serving	Kcal	Fat	Saturates	Carbs	Sugars	Fibre	Protein	Salt
	348	7g	1g	51g	9g	4g	14g	0.6g

BIG MEALS & ENTERTAINING

This chapter is for the bigger families, or those of us who like to share the food as well as the love. Eating on a budget doesn't mean you can't entertain, as you'll see from these healthy and delicious crowd-pleasing recipes. All of these use cheaper cuts of meat, such as chicken thighs, or include protein-rich and filling beans and pulses or fresh and vibrant vegetables to make that packet of mince go a little bit further. Let's get the party started . . .

TURKEY AND FENNEL PATTIES

Turkey mince is a great-value meat that has a mild taste, so it's the perfect base for other flavours. It is also low in fat, so it's a much healthier variation on the usual meat patties. The deliciously aniseedy fennel lifts these from being simple burgers to something you can confidently serve to guests. It's the ideal light dish for a summery evening – cherry tomatoes are in season then, so get the freshest ones you can.

SERVES 8

4 tablespoons olive oil
1 onion, peeled and finely chopped
1 fennel bulb, cored and finely chopped
750g turkey mince
1 slice of brown bread, blitzed into breadcrumbs in a food processor
3 tablespoons fresh chives, chopped
200g red cherry tomatoes
200g yellow cherry tomatoes
2 tablespoons extra virgin olive oil
2 tablespoons balsamic glaze
Salt and freshly ground black pepper

1. Pour 1 tablespoon of the oil into a medium saucepan and place over a medium heat. Fry the onions with the fennel for 10 minutes, stirring occasionally with a wooden spoon. Remove from the heat and set aside.

2. Put the turkey, breadcrumbs and chives into a large bowl and season with salt and pepper. Add the onion and fennel and mix to combine. Form the mixture into 8 patties and set aside.

3. Preheat the oven to 180°C/gas mark 4.

4. Pour the remaining oil into a large (30cm) non-stick frying pan and place over a high heat. Fry the patties for 10 minutes, turning halfway through. Transfer the patties to a baking tray and bake in the oven for 10 minutes.

5. Meanwhile, put the cherry tomatoes into a medium bowl and pour over the extra virgin olive oil and balsamic glaze. Season with salt and pepper and stir all together.

6. Serve the turkey patties on a large serving platter surrounded by the cherry tomato salad.

GINO'S TIP: If you keep your fresh tomatoes in the fridge, allow them to come to room temperature before serving – they will have a better flavour.

Per serving	Kcal	Fat	Saturates	Carbs	Sugars	Fibre	Protein	Salt
	213	9g	1g	7g	5g	2g	24g	0.2g

FRITTATA WITH POTATOES, LEEKS AND TALEGGIO CHEESE

Who says frittata has to be for lunch or a simple supper? Cut into wedges and served with a fabulous big green salad, this is the perfect sharing dish for an informal supper with friends. Taleggio is a cheese that comes from an area bearing the same name in Northern Italy and, as well as being popular on a cheeseboard, it is also much-used in Italian cookery because it melts so beautifully when heated. It has a mild, fruity flavour, which holds its own with the stronger leeks and chives.

SERVES 8

3 potatoes (about 600g in total), peeled
50g salted butter
1 large leek (about 350g), thinly sliced
15 medium eggs
4 tablespoons chives, finely chopped
120g Taleggio cheese
Salt and freshly ground black pepper

1. Cut the potatoes in half and put into a medium saucepan. Cover with cold water and bring to the boil over a high heat. Reduce the heat to medium and cook for 20 minutes or until tender when poked with the end of a knife. Drain and set aside to cool slightly.

2. Melt the butter in a large (30cm) non-stick frying pan over a medium heat. Add the leek and fry for 5 minutes, stirring occasionally with a wooden spoon.

3. Meanwhile, slice the cooked potatoes into 5mm slices and set aside. Beat the eggs in a medium bowl, season with 1 teaspoon of salt and stir in the chives.

4. Preheat the grill to high.

5. Spread the leeks evenly over the base of the frying pan and add the potato slices in an even layer. Break the Taleggio cheese into small pieces and dot over the potato. Reduce the heat to medium and pour the egg around all the potatoes as evenly as you can. Cook for 12 minutes, gently moving the eggs around after 3 minutes, then 6 minutes.

6. Transfer the frying pan to the grill and continue to cook for 3 minutes or until golden brown and cooked through.

7. Season with pepper and serve with a simple green salad dressed with extra virgin olive oil and red wine vinegar.

GINO'S TIP: If you have one, a mandolin is great for getting the potatoes evenly sliced and nice and thin, meaning they will cook quicker.

Per serving	Kcal	Fat	Saturates	Carbs	Sugars	Fibre	Protein	Salt
	303	19g	8g	14g	2g	2g	18g	1.6g

ROAST CHICKEN THIGHS WITH ROOT VEGETABLES AND WHOLEGRAIN MUSTARD

Chicken thighs are a cheap, tasty way to cook for a crowd. This easy one-pot dish is like a Sunday lunch in one and, better still, all the flavours beautifully infuse the ingredients, so you don't need to worry about complementary side dishes. Just shove it in the oven and spend that all-important time with your family or guests rather than in the kitchen.

SERVES 6

1 large parsnip (about 250g), peeled and cut into 3cm chunks
1 swede (about 750g), peeled and cut into 3cm chunks
2 large carrots (about 250g), peeled and cut into 3cm discs
500g new potatoes, washed but not peeled
4 tablespoons runny honey
1 tablespoon wholegrain mustard
3 teaspoons fresh rosemary leaves
2 onions, peeled and roughly chopped
1.5kg chicken thighs, fat trimmed
100ml olive oil
100ml hot chicken stock
Salt and freshly ground black pepper

1. Preheat the oven to 200°C/gas mark 6.

2. Put the parsnip, swede, carrots and potatoes into a large saucepan. Cover with cold water and bring to the boil. Reduce the heat to medium and cook for 5 minutes, then drain and return to the pan.

3. Mix the honey, mustard and rosemary together in a small bowl and pour over the vegetables. Stir all together.

4. Divide the onions between 2 roasting tins measuring about 35 x 25cm. Nestle the chicken thighs around the onions and tip in the vegetables so that everything is evenly distributed. Pour half the oil and half the chicken stock into each tin and season well with salt and pepper. Mix to combine.

5. Cover the roasting tins with foil and roast in the oven for 20 minutes, then remove the foil and continue to cook for 30 minutes. At this point take the roasting tins out of the oven and turn the vegetables over. Return to the oven for a final 20 minutes.

6. Serve immediately.

GINO'S TIP: To reduce the calories, remove the skin from the chicken – but it tastes amazing!

Per serving	Kcal	Fat	Saturates	Carbs	Sugars	Fibre	Protein	Salt
	693	43g	9g	36g	21g	8g	37g	0.6g

STUFFED COURGETTES WITH TOMATOES, GORGONZOLA AND OLIVES

A light, healthy main that has maximum impact for minimum effort. Courgettes make ideal cases to load up with really strong flavours . . . so it's got to be more chilli! The creamy Gorgonzola softens the heat slightly, but adds its own strong impact, melting and oozing all over the plate. *Fantastico!*

SERVES 8

8 courgettes
4 tablespoons olive oil
2 red onions, peeled and
   finely chopped
1 x 400g tin of chopped
   tomatoes
1 tablespoon tomato purée
1 teaspoon dried chilli flakes
100g pitted green olives in
   brine, drained and
   roughly chopped
100g Gorgonzola cheese
Salt

1. Preheat the oven to 190°C/gas mark 5.

2. Cut the courgettes in half lengthways and scoop out the flesh with a teaspoon. Place the courgette boats onto 2 large baking trays. Finely chop the scooped out flesh and set aside.

3. Brush the hollowed out courgettes with 2 tablespoons of oil and bake in the middle of the oven for 10 minutes. Remove from the oven and set aside.

4. Pour the remaining oil into a medium frying pan, add the onions and fry the onions over a medium heat for 5 minutes, stirring occasionally with a wooden spoon. Add the reserved courgette flesh and continue to fry for 3 minutes.

5. Pour in the tomatoes, tomato purée and chilli flakes and season with salt; mix all together. Bring to the boil then reduce the heat to low and continue to cook for 8 minutes, stirring occasionally.

6. Spoon half of the tomato sauce into the halved courgettes. Sprinkle over the olives, then dot with the Gorgonzola cheese as evenly as possible. Spoon the remaining tomato sauce over the courgettes. Bake in the middle of the oven for 15 minutes.

7. Serve immediately with a simple mixed salad dressed with extra virgin olive oil and balsamic vinegar.

Per serving	Kcal	Fat	Saturates	Carbs	Sugars	Fibre	Protein	Salt
	167	11g	4g	8g	7g	4g	7g	0.8g

CHILLI CON CARNE WITH FRESH ROSEMARY

A good chilli is a brilliant crowd-pleaser, popular with both kids and adults, and perfect for an autumn afternoon or after a cold winter walk. In Italy we use a lot of beans to bulk out meals because it means you can use less expensive meat to stretch a meal and feed more people. Chilli is often made with kidney beans, but I love using the Italian staples – creamy borlotti beans and nutty chickpeas. Light the fire, open the wine and relax and enjoy!

SERVES 6–8

3 tablespoons olive oil
2 red onions, peeled and finely chopped
2 carrots, peeled and finely chopped
2 celery sticks, finely chopped
1 tablespoon fresh rosemary leaves, finely chopped
2 yellow peppers, deseeded and finely chopped
2½ teaspoons dried chilli flakes
1½ teaspoons hot paprika
750g beef mince
2 x 400g tins of chopped tomatoes
1 x 400g tin of borlotti beans, drained
1 x 400g tin of chickpeas, drained and rinsed
200ml hot beef stock
3 tablespoons fresh flat-leaf parsley, chopped
Salt

1. Pour the oil into a large saucepan and place over a medium heat. Fry the onions, carrots, celery and rosemary for 8 minutes, stirring occasionally with a wooden spoon.

2. Add the peppers and cook for 3 minutes, followed by the chilli flakes and paprika; cook for 2 minutes. Tip in the beef mince and continue to cook for a further 10 minutes, stirring occasionally to break up the meat as much as you can.

3. Stir in the tomatoes, borlotti beans, chickpeas and stock. Season with salt and bring to the boil, then reduce the heat to low. Continue to cook, partially covered with a lid, for 35 minutes, stirring every 10 minutes or so.

4. Stir in the parsley and serve with plain boiled rice.

GINO'S TIP: If you want a really hearty, filling meal, you could serve this chilli with some gnocchi, Italian-style!

Per serving	Kcal	Fat	Saturates	Carbs	Sugars	Fibre	Protein	Salt
	502	28g	10g	24g	12g	10g	34g	0.6g

OVEN-BAKED FISH CAKES WITH SMOKED PAPRIKA

It's so easy to make your own fish cakes and, believe me; once you've done it you'll wonder why you hadn't done it before. These are brilliant because they cut out the oil and mess of frying and instead just get baked in the oven. They're surprisingly filling and very elegant, so you just need some salad to accompany them – nothing more.

SERVES 6

700g potatoes, peeled and
    cut into small chunks
60g salted butter
350g skinless salmon fillet
100ml semi-skimmed milk
1 slice of brown bread,
    blitzed into breadcrumbs
    in a food processor
1 teaspoon smoked paprika
3 tablespoons fresh flat-leaf
    parsley, finely chopped
1 large egg, beaten
30g plain flour
70g rocket leaves
Salt

1. Put the potatoes into a medium saucepan, cover with cold water and bring to the boil. Reduce the heat to medium and continue to cook for 15 minutes or until the potatoes are tender when poked with a fork. Drain and tip back in the same pan. Season with salt and add half the butter. Mash until smooth and set aside.

2. Meanwhile, put the salmon into a small saucepan and pour over the milk and 100ml water. Bring to the boil, reduce the heat and continue to cook for 10 minutes. Drain and flake the fish into the potatoes.

3. Preheat the oven to 200°C/gas mark 6 and line a baking tray with baking parchment.

4. Add the breadcrumbs, smoked paprika, parsley and egg to the potato and salmon mixture. Season with salt and mix all together, then form the mixture into 12 fish cakes. Put the flour onto a flat plate. Roll the fish cakes in the flour and place onto the baking tray. Melt the remaining butter and brush over the cakes, coating both sides.

5. Bake into the oven for 7 minutes, then carefully turn each fish cake and return to the oven for a further 7 minutes.

6. Serve on a bed of rocket leaves with a bottle of chilled Prosecco.

GINO'S TIP: These are a great way to use up leftover mash!

Per serving	Kcal	Fat	Saturates	Carbs	Sugars	Fibre	Protein	Salt
	345	18g	7g	26g	2g	3g	17g	0.4g

SPICY LAMB BURGERS WITH HERBED YOGURT

For burgers, lamb makes a really nice change from beef. These need to be prepared ahead and rested in the fridge to make sure they don't fall apart when they are cooked, so they're a great make-ahead meal. The yogurt makes a lovely cooling accompaniment to the spicy burgers. Light that barbecue and open the cold beers . . .

SERVES 6

600g lamb mince
½ red onion, peeled and grated
3 tablespoons fresh flat-leaf parsley, finely chopped
1 carrot, peeled and grated
1 teaspoon hot paprika
2 teaspoons dried chilli flakes
1 large egg, beaten
2 slices of brown bread, blitzed into breadcrumbs in a food processor
6 burger buns
60g rocket leaves
Salt

For the herbed yogurt
200g Greek yogurt
3 tablespoons fresh flat-leaf parsley, finely chopped
10 mint leaves, finely chopped
Salt

1. Put the lamb, onion, parsley, carrot, paprika, chilli flakes, egg and breadcrumbs into a large bowl. Season with 1 teaspoon of salt. Using your hands, mix well to combine and shape into 6 burgers. Place the burgers onto a flat plate, cover with cling film and rest in the fridge for 1 hour.

2. To make the herbed yogurt, put the yogurt and herbs into a medium bowl and stir to combine. Season with salt and set aside.

3. Remove the burgers from the fridge 10 minutes before you want to cook them.

4. Preheat the grill to high and line a large baking tray with baking parchment. Put the burgers onto the lined tray and cook under the grill for 5 minutes, then gently turn each burger and continue to cook for a further 5 minutes.

5. Meanwhile, split the burger buns in half and toast them.

6. Serve the burgers between the buns with rocket leaves and a dollop of the herbed yogurt. Fantastic served with cold beers.

GINO'S TIP: If you're short of time, place the burger patties in the freezer for 10 minutes to firm them up before frying.

Per serving	Kcal	Fat	Saturates	Carbs	Sugars	Fibre	Protein	Salt
	510	21g	9g	46g	5g	4g	32g	2.5g

SPICY MINCED PORK STEW WITH RED PEPPERS AND PEAS

Minced pork makes a great substitute for other minced meats, particularly the richer beef, but it often gets overlooked. It is just as versatile as other minced meats but has a lighter flavour than beef and works really well with spicy ingredients. In Italy we tend to use it a lot in combination with other minced meats for a deeper flavour. With beans, peas and veg, this is a great all-in-one dish and easily keeps a crowd happy.

SERVES 6–8

2 tablespoons olive oil
2 red onions, peeled and finely chopped
1 carrot, peeled and finely chopped
2 red peppers, deseeded and roughly chopped
750g pork mince
2 x 400g tins of chopped tomatoes
2 x 400g tins of cannellini beans, drained
1 tablespoon tomato purée
4 teaspoons chilli powder
150g frozen peas, defrosted
3 tablespoons chives, chopped
Salt

1. Pour the oil into a large saucepan and place over a medium heat. Fry the onions and carrot for 5 minutes, stirring occasionally with a wooden spoon. Add the peppers and continue to fry for 2 minutes, stirring.

2. Tip in the pork mince and continue to cook for 10 minutes, breaking the meat up with the wooden spoon.

3. Stir in the tinned tomatoes, cannellini beans, tomato purée, chilli powder and 2 teaspoons of salt. Bring to the boil, then reduce the heat to low and continue to cook for 15 minutes. Stir occasionally.

4. Add the peas and chives and cook for a further 15 minutes, stirring occasionally.

5. Spoon over a jacket potato or serve with warm crusty bread.

GINO'S TIP: If you are getting your mince from a butcher, ask them to use half pork belly and half shoulder, which gives the best blend of fat and flavour.

Per serving	Kcal	Fat	Saturates	Carbs	Sugars	Fibre	Protein	Salt
	407	17g	5g	24g	13g	11g	34g	0.5g

CHICKEN AND LEEK PIE WITH FILO PASTRY TOPPING

To give that wow factor to a pie, try filo pastry, rather than the traditional crust. The delicate scrunched layers gently rise and separate, turning an appetising golden brown. Filo pastry is also much lower in saturated fat, making this a healthy version as well as adding a wonderful crunch. It's a pie that needs a little preparation, but it's pretty simple really and well worth the effort for the amazing compliments you will get from your guests.

SERVES 6

800ml chicken stock
2 garlic cloves, peeled and crushed
2 carrots (about 350g), peeled and roughly chopped
500g skinless and boneless chicken thighs
3 tablespoons olive oil
1 large leek (about 300g), thinly sliced
2 celery sticks, roughly chopped
100g closed cup mushrooms, thinly sliced
2 tablespoons fresh thyme leaves
3 tablespoons cornflour, mixed with 5 tablespoons cold water
4 tablespoons reduced-fat mascarpone cheese
1 teaspoon English mustard
3 x 40g sheets of frozen filo pastry, defrosted
Salt and freshly ground black pepper

1. Pour the stock into a large (30cm) lidded non-stick frying pan. Bring to the boil and add the garlic and carrots. Reduce the heat to low and cook for 3 minutes. Add the chicken thighs, cover and cook for a further 15 minutes, stirring occasionally.

2. Meanwhile, pour 2 tablespoons of the oil into a medium saucepan and place over a medium heat. Add the leek and fry for 5 minutes, stirring occasionally. Add the celery and mushrooms and cook for 3 minutes, stirring. Stir in the thyme and season well. Remove from the heat and tip the vegetables into a 2-litre pie dish.

3. Remove the chicken from the stock with a slotted spoon and, when cool enough to handle, cut into bite-sized pieces. Scatter the chicken over the vegetables in the pie dish, then preheat the oven to 180°C/ gas mark 4. Pass the stock through a sieve into the pan that you cooked the leeks in. Add the carrots and garlic from the sieve to the chicken and vegetables in the pie dish.

4. Heat the stock over a low heat. Very slowly pour in the cornflour, whisking all the time with a balloon whisk. Continue to heat and whisk for 5 minutes until the sauce starts to thicken. Remove from the heat and stir in the mascarpone and mustard. Pour the sauce over the vegetables and chicken and gently stir.

5. Cut each sheet of filo pastry into 4. Brush each one with the remaining oil and then roughly scrunch each square. Arrange them evenly over the chicken and vegetables and then transfer the pie to the oven. Bake for 30 minutes until golden on top. Serve immediately.

GINO'S TIP: You need to work quickly when you are using filo pastry. While you lay out one sheet, keep the others covered with a damp cloth to stop them drying out.

Per serving	Kcal	Fat	Saturates	Carbs	Sugars	Fibre	Protein	Salt
	371	18g	6g	24g	6g	5g	26g	0.7g

MUSHROOM STEW WITH MASCARPONE AND MUSTARD

So you've got guests arriving any minute and you've only just walked through the door. How do you get a hearty, warming meal for six on the table when you're up against the clock? This stew is the answer. Chestnut mushrooms have a firm, meaty texture that makes them perfect for casseroles and they impart a strong, rich flavour, too. You won't find you're missing the meat here and it doesn't need a long cooking time to get the same effect. Dinner? Done.

SERVES 6

60g salted butter
4 tablespoons olive oil
2 red onions, peeled and thinly sliced
500g chestnut mushrooms, sliced
1 x 390g tin of artichoke hearts in water, drained and cut into quarters
3 tablespoons wholegrain mustard
250g reduced-fat mascarpone cheese
100ml hot vegetable stock
10 yellow cherry tomatoes, cut into quarters
4 tablespoons fresh flat-leaf parsley, chopped
Salt and freshly ground black pepper

1. Put the butter and oil into a large saucepan and place over a medium heat. Add the onions and fry for 6 minutes, stirring occasionally with a wooden spoon. Add the mushrooms and cook for 8 minutes, stirring occasionally.

2. Stir in the artichokes, mustard, mascarpone cheese and vegetable stock. Season well with salt and pepper. Reduce the heat to low and cook for 18 minutes, stirring occasionally

3. Stir through the cherry tomatoes and parsley and serve immediately with toasted ciabatta bread rubbed with fresh garlic.

GINO'S TIP: Make a double batch and the next day top with puff pastry, brush with egg wash and bake, for a beautiful mushroom pie.

Per serving	Kcal	Fat	Saturates	Carbs	Sugars	Fibre	Protein	Salt
	310	26g	12g	9g	5g	3g	8g	0.8g

PUDDINGS
& TREATS

Everybody needs a treat every now and then and eating healthily doesn't mean completely cutting out the sweet things in life. In this chapter you'll find healthier versions of one of my personal favourite puddings – ice cream – as well as crunchy biscuits and moreish cakes perfect for serving with coffee, not to mention gorgeously fruity puds and more indulgent chocolatey treats. Some of these are everyday delicious, while others you might want to keep for special occasions. Whatever you choose, these home-made treats will be served up to smiles all round.

YOGURT ICE CREAM WITH BERRIES AND HONEY

A fantastically easy ice cream – there's no whipping of cream needed; just toss all the ingredients into a blender, whizz and freeze! Using yogurt is also much healthier than using cream and frozen berries will get you closer to achieving your five-a-day, so this is a good one for the kids. Ok, it's not the traditional Italian gelato . . . but it's every bit as good.

SERVES 4

500g frozen mixed berries
 (I used blackberries,
 cherries, strawberries,
 raspberries, blackcurrants
 and redcurrants)
500g low-fat Greek yogurt
5 tablespoons runny honey
 (or to taste)
1 tablespoon vanilla extract

1. Put the berries, yogurt, honey and vanilla into a food processer and blitz until smooth. Taste the mixture, as it might need a little extra honey.

2. Pour into a 1-litre freezerproof lidded container and transfer to the freezer for 3 hours.

3. Remove from the freezer 10–15 minutes before you want to serve this to soften slightly. Scoop into bowls and serve with a little biscuit on the side.

GINO'S TIP: You can use other frozen fruit here if you want a variety of flavours.

Per serving	Kcal	Fat	Saturates	Carbs	Sugars	Fibre	Protein	Salt
	232	4g	3g	36g	36g	4g	8g	0.3g

LIME AND FRESH BASIL SORBET

This is a real tongue-tingler; the zesty limes and fresh basil leaves are perfectly matched and this makes an unusual and delicious variation on lemon sorbet. Serve this on a hot summer's day or after a spicy meal to cool your mouth – or you could even serve it between courses to cleanse and refresh the palate if you were feeling particularly indulgent . . .

SERVES 6

400g caster sugar
10 limes
20g basil leaves, plus
   6 leaves to garnish

1. Tip the sugar into a medium saucepan and pour over 400ml cold water. Using a potato peeler, peel the zest from 2 of the limes in strips and add to the pan. Place the pan over a medium heat and bring to the boil. Continue to boil for 1 minute then remove from the heat and discard the peel from the sugar syrup. Set aside.

2. Juice the limes, including the ones with the peel removed, and pour into the sugar syrup. Add the basil leaves and use a hand-held blender to whizz until smooth.

3. Pour the mixture into a 1-litre freezerproof, lidded container and transfer to the freezer for 4 hours. Remove from the freezer and blend again, preferably in a blender if you have one. If not, then use the hand-held blender. Return to the freezer for 3 hours.

4. Spoon into glasses and serve garnished with basil on top.

GINO'S TIP: This sorbet is more like an Italian granita, but with a rougher texture. If you prefer a smoother texture, make this in an ice-cream machine, if you have one.

Per serving	Kcal	Fat	Saturates	Carbs	Sugars	Fibre	Protein	Salt
	271	0.1g	0g	67g	67g	0g	0.2g	0g

CHOCOLATE MOUSSE WITH AMARETTO LIQUEUR AND BLACK PEPPER

A good meal should always be followed by a good dessert – and this is just that. You may be familiar with the combination of chocolate and salt . . . but pepper? Trust me, it's fantastic; it gives a little heat and spiciness to this rich mousse. It also makes a brilliant combination with the amaretto; amaretto means 'a little bitter' and it perfectly describes this almond-flavoured liqueur. This is definitely a dessert for the grown-ups!

SERVES 6

200g dark chocolate
4 medium eggs, separated
50g caster sugar
4 tablespoons Amaretto liqueur
½ fine ground black pepper
250g fresh raspberries
Icing sugar for dusting

1. Put the chocolate into a heatproof bowl and melt over a pan of simmering water, ensuring that the base of the bowl does not touch the water. Set aside to cool but not harden.

2. Put the egg whites into a very clean and dry medium bowl. Using a hand-held electric whisk, whisk until stiff. Add the sugar one teaspoon at a time, whisking all the time. Set aside.

3. In a separate medium bowl beat the eggs yolks together with the Amaretto liqueur and black pepper.

4. Pour the melted chocolate into the egg yolks and whisk together until thoroughly combined.

5. Using a large metal spoon, add the egg whites into the chocolate mixture, gently folding all the ingredients together until no white remains, taking care not to knock out all the air.

6. Divide the raspberries between 6 dessert glasses, reserving 18 of them for decoration. Pour the chocolate mixture over the raspberries and cover with cling film. Leave to rest into the fridge for 3 hours until set.

7. Just before serving, remove the cling film and decorate the mousses with the reserved raspberries, 3 for each mousse. Sprinkle the top with a little icing sugar and serve.

Per serving	Kcal	Fat	Saturates	Carbs	Sugars	Fibre	Protein	Salt
	321	18g	9g	24g	20g	5g	8g	0.2g

BAKED APPLES WITH NUTTY FILO DISCS

I love apple strudel. Now, you may think that it is an Austrian dessert – and you'd be right. But it is also very popular in Northern Italy. I could eat it all the time, but all those layers of pastry aren't the healthiest dessert option, so I created this. I guess you could say it's a sort of upside-down, open strudel. The nuts and baked filo add a wonderful crunch against the softened apple.

SERVES 4

40g walnuts, finely chopped
40g roasted hazelnuts, finely
  chopped
40g demerara sugar
1 teaspoon mixed spice, plus
  2 large pinches
3 sheets of filo pastry,
  measuring about 25 x 35cm
60g salted butter, melted,
  plus one generous knob
4 Granny Smith apples,
  cored
1 teaspoon caster sugar
75g reduced-fat crème
  fraîche, to serve
10g icing sugar, to serve

1. Mix the walnuts, hazelnuts, demerara sugar and 1 teaspoon of the mixed spice in a small bowl. Set aside.

2. Line a large baking tray measuring about 40 x 30cm with baking parchment. Place a sheet of filo pastry onto the baking parchment and brush with some of the melted butter. Turn the filo over and brush the other side with butter. Sprinkle half of the nut mixture over the pastry and lay another filo sheet over the nuts. Again, brush the sheet with butter and sprinkle over the remaining nuts. Place the final sheet of filo on top and brush with the remaining melted butter. Place another sheet of baking parchment over the filo and lay a baking tray that is about the same size as the filo sheets on top of the parchment. Transfer to the fridge for 30 minutes.

3. Preheat the oven to 160°C/gas mark 3. Remove the filo from the fridge. Take off the top baking tray and carefully roll back the top sheet of parchment. Using an 8cm cookie cutter, cut 8 discs in the pastry, leaving them on the tray. Remove the offcuts. Replace the reserved baking parchment on the nutty discs and place the smaller tray back on the paper. Bake in the oven for 8 minutes or until golden brown. Remove from the oven and leave to cool slightly without taking off the paper and top tray. Set aside.

4. Increase the oven temperature to 180°C/gas mark 4. Trim the apples at the top and bottom. Place a medium ovenproof pan over a medium heat and melt the remaining knob of butter. Sprinkle over the sugar and add the apples, flat side down. Cook for 10 minutes, turning halfway through. Transfer to the oven for 10 minutes. Combine the crème fraîche, icing sugar and remaining pinches of mixed spice in a small bowl and set aside in the fridge.

5. To serve, place a nutty disc onto each serving plate followed by an apple then another disc on top. Spoon over the buttery apple juices from the pan, add a dollop of crème fraîche and dust with icing sugar. Serve immediately.

Per serving	Kcal 523	Fat 35g	Saturates 14g	Carbs 43g	Sugars 26g	Fibre 3g	Protein 7g	Salt 0.7g

COFFEE AND VANILLA MARBLE CAKE

In Italy, cake is served with coffee, not tea; and we dunk chunks of it into our espresso until it is lightly soaked and the flavours have permeated the sponge. We are particularly keen on cake for breakfast, so you will often see locals scoffing it in cafés before work! Marble cake is a clever way of combining different tastes and creating something that looks fantastic cut into slices, too.

SERVES 10

250g salted butter, softened, plus extra for greasing
4½ heaped teaspoons instant coffee granules
250g caster sugar
4 medium eggs
250g self-raising flour
2 teaspoons baking powder
Pinch of salt
1½ teaspoons vanilla extract
50g icing sugar

1. Preheat the oven to 180°C/gas mark 4 and lightly grease a 23cm savarin mould with butter.

2. Dissolve 3 teaspoons of the coffee granules in 2 tablespoons of boiling water and set aside to cool.

3. Put the butter, sugar, eggs, flour, baking powder and salt into a medium bowl and beat until smooth. Transfer half the mixture to another bowl. Add the dissolved coffee to one of the bowls and beat to combine, then add the vanilla to the other bowl and beat to combine.

4. Using up all the batter drop tablespoons of the vanilla mixture evenly spaced around the edge of the mould. Now drop tablespoons of the coffee mixture in between the vanilla. Using a table knife, gently swirl the mixture together.

5. Bake in the oven for 40 minutes or until a skewer inserted into the cake comes out clean. Leave in the tin to cool for a few minutes then turn out onto a wire rack to cool completely.

6. To make the icing, dissolve the remaining coffee with 2 tablespoons of boiling water in a small bowl. Add the icing sugar and stir to form a runny icing. Drizzle over the top and down the sides of the cake.

7. Cut into slices and serve with little cups of espresso coffee.

GINO'S TIP: Make sure there are no gaps between the different cake mixes; if you think there may be too many air bubbles, tap the base of the tin gently on the work surface to even out the mixture before baking.

Per serving	Kcal 431	Fat 23g	Saturates 14g	Carbs 49g	Sugars 30g	Fibre 1g	Protein 6g	Salt 1.1g

CHOCOLATE AND NUT FINGER BISCUITS

These biscottini are a simplified version of the traditional twice-baked biscotti. The fingers are slightly drier than the biscuits that non-Italians are used to, but so delicious! They are perfect for serving either with ice cream or as the Italians eat them, dipped into a morning caffe or a chilled sweet dessert wine.

SERVES 8

2 egg whites
110g caster sugar
60g roasted and ground
   hazelnuts
100g ground almonds
15g plain flour
15g cocoa powder
35g plain chocolate
35g white chocolate

1. Preheat the oven to 160°C/gas mark 3 and line 2 baking trays with baking parchment.

2. Using a hand-held electric whisk, whisk the egg whites in a medium bowl until thick and foamy. Add the sugar, a teaspoon at a time, and whisk until all the sugar has been incorporated into the egg whites. Add the hazelnuts and almonds and sift over the flour and cocoa powder. Fold until well combined.

3. Spoon the mixture into a medium freezer bag. Push the mixture into the corner and, using a pair of scissors, make a cut about the size of a 10p coin, cutting off the corner. Pipe long fingers onto the baking parchment, about 10cm long. You should have made 16 fingers. Bake in the oven for 10 minutes. Remove from the oven and leave to cool on the trays.

4. Once cool, move the fingers close together side by side in a line. Put the plain chocolate into the corner of a small food bag and do the same with the white chocolate in a separate bag. Put the bag of plain chocolate into a microwave for 50 seconds to melt the chocolate. Take care not to over-heat the chocolate so check after 30 seconds and continue for 10 seconds at a time until just melted. Do the same with the white chocolate.

5. Push the chocolate into the corner of the bag and make a tiny cut. Do this next to the fingers, as the chocolate will spurt out. Now drizzle both the plain and white chocolate over the fingers until all the melted chocolate is used up.

6. Transfer to the fridge for 15 minutes to set, then arrange on a serving plate and serve, with ice cream or simply on their own for a delicious treat.

GINO'S TIP: If you like, you can swap the hazelnuts for almonds or pistachios.

Per serving	Kcal	Fat	Saturates	Carbs	Sugars	Fibre	Protein	Salt
	248	15g	3g	22g	20g	1g	6g	0.1g

STRAWBERRY AND MASCARPONE TARTS WITH LIMONCELLO

For me, limoncello is the scent and flavour of home. Traditionally, this citrus liqueur is made from the best lemons in the world – Sorrento lemons. In Italy it is a hugely popular drink, with many people in the south making their own version. It's really strong, about 40% proof, so you only need a small amount. Here, limoncello is mixed with creamy Italian cheeses and fresh seasonal strawberries in a filo case. Absolute heaven . . .

SERVES 4

35g salted butter, melted
2 x 40g sheets of filo pastry, each cut into 8 squares
30g icing sugar, sifted, plus extra for decoration
Large pinch of ground cinnamon
75g mascarpone cheese
75g ricotta cheese
Grated zest of ½ unwaxed lemon
½ teaspoon vanilla extract
1 tablespoon limoncello liqueur
100g or 8 strawberries, hulled and sliced

1. Preheat the oven to 180°C/gas mark 4 and brush 4 holes of a muffin tin with a little of the melted butter.

2. Lay out all the squares of filo pastry. Brush them evenly with the melted butter and sift over 10g of the icing sugar. Sprinkle with the cinnamon.

3. Line each greased muffin tin hole with 4 squares of filo pastry, each arranged at slightly different angles. Press the pastry down into the hole to create a cup. Transfer to the oven and bake for 8 minutes until golden brown and crispy. Remove from the oven and set aside to cool.

4. Meanwhile, put the mascarpone, ricotta, lemon zest, vanilla extract, limoncello and the remaining icing sugar into a medium bowl. Using a hand-held electric whisk, beat until smooth.

5. Put the filo cups onto a serving platter and evenly spoon in the mascarpone mixture.

6. Arrange the sliced strawberries on top of the mascarpone cream and sprinkle over a little icing sugar to serve.

GINO'S TIP: To get the very best flavours from limoncello it must be served really cold. Keep your bottle in the freezer so it's always ready to use.

Per serving	Kcal	Fat	Saturates	Carbs	Sugars	Fibre	Protein	Salt
	285	18g	11g	22g	11g	2g	4g	0.4g

QUICK BANANA AND NUTELLA ICE CREAM

This is one that the kids always love. It's real nursery food – banana and Nutella . . . mmmmm. With only five ingredients, this is so easy that you won't mind whipping it up for them whenever they demand it – which might be often, once they've tried it! Banana has such a creamy texture when blended that you don't need cream here – and it is also packed with potassium, which has been associated with lowering blood pressure. So this is almost good for you, then!

SERVES 4

5 ripe bananas
5 tablespoons semi-skimmed milk
1 tablespoon vanilla extract
125g Nutella chocolate and hazelnut spread
30g dark chocolate chips

1. Cut the bananas into small chunks and place in the freezer until frozen, at least 4 hours.

2. Tip the frozen bananas into a powerful blender with the milk and vanilla extract. Blend until smooth. Add the Nutella and blend again until all combined.

3. Pour into a 1-litre freezerproof lidded container and transfer to the freezer for 4 hours.

4. To make sure the ice cream is smooth and creamy, remove from the freezer 15 minutes before you want to serve it. Scoop into bowls and sprinkle over the chocolate chips.

GINO'S TIP: Use a really good blender to make this, so that you can get the mixture really smooth before freezing – you don't want lumps of ice.

Per serving	Kcal	Fat	Saturates	Carbs	Sugars	Fibre	Protein	Salt
	223	9g	4g	30g	27g	3g	3g	0g

COURGETTE AND WALNUT LOAF CAKE WITH DELICIOUS LEMON ICING

For any of you gardeners who get the inevitable glut of courgettes in the summer – this cake is for you. The grated courgette is not just a healthy addition to up your greens intake, but it also keeps the sponge amazingly moist. Just make sure you drain them really well, or else they can make the cake soggy. The walnuts add a wonderful crunch to each slice. You can eat this one with tea!

SERVES 10

250g courgettes
2 medium eggs
125ml corn oil
250g golden caster sugar
Grated zest of 1 unwaxed
   lemon, plus 2 tablespoons
   of the lemon juice
75g sultanas
½ teaspoon vanilla extract
380g self-raising flour
1 teaspoon ground cinnamon
½ teaspoon table salt
60g walnut pieces, roughly
   chopped
50g icing sugar

1. Preheat the oven to 180°C/gas mark 4 and lightly oil and line a 1kg loaf tin with a strip of baking parchment.

2. Finely grate the courgettes and put into a sieve set over a sink or bowl. Leave for 30 minutes then squeeze out as much liquid as you can with your hands.

3. Using an electric mixer beat the eggs in a large bowl until foamy. Add the corn oil, caster sugar, lemon zest, sultanas, vanilla extract and courgettes. Briefly beat with the mixer to combine.

4. Add the flour, cinnamon and salt. Using a large spoon stir thoroughly then fold in the walnuts.

5. Pour the mixture into the prepared loaf tin and transfer to the oven for 1 hour or until a skewer inserted into the cake comes out clean. Lightly wrap the top of the cake with foil for the last 10 minutes of cooking to prevent burning. Remove from the oven, discard the foil top and leave to cool in the tin before turning out onto a serving plate.

6. Sift the icing sugar into a small bowl. Pass the lemon juice through the sieve into the icing sugar. Stir to combine and then drizzle over the cake.

7. Cut into slices and serve with a nice cup of tea.

GINO'S TIP: Make sure you squeeze out as much of the moisture from the courgettes as you can. Use your hands, or grate the courgettes onto a clean tea towel and then squeeze over a sink.

Per serving	Kcal	Fat	Saturates	Carbs	Sugars	Fibre	Protein	Salt
	456	18g	3g	64g	36g	2g	7g	0.62g

SPICED GRAPE CAKE WITH ORANGE ZEST

Grape cake is a rustic Italian bake, which is traditionally made during the grape harvest when the fruits are in abundance. It can be eaten at any time of day – even as a dessert with a glass of Vin Santo. The combination of butter and oil makes this a really light cake and very, very moreish.

SERVES 10

75g salted butter, softened
150g light muscovado sugar
2 medium eggs
Grated zest of 1 orange
½ teaspoon nutmeg
1 teaspoon ground cinnamon
50ml semi-skimmed milk
120ml olive oil
150g plain flour
1 teaspoon baking powder
150g red seedless grapes,
   halved lengthways
2 heaped tablespoons
   demerara sugar

1. Preheat the oven to 170°C/gas mark 3 and line a 20cm round loose-bottomed cake tin with baking parchment.

2. Whisk the butter and sugar together in a medium bowl until creamy and well combined. Whisk in the eggs, one at a time. Add the orange zest, nutmeg and cinnamon, pour in the milk and olive oil and whisk to combine.

3. Tip in the flour and baking powder and give it a final beat.

4. Pour the mixture into the prepared tin and evenly scatter over the grapes. Sprinkle with the demerara sugar and bake in the oven for 45 minutes or until a skewer inserted into the cake comes out clean. Remove from the oven and leave in the tin to cool.

5. Once cool, remove from the tin and slide onto a serving plate. Serve with your mid-morning coffee or afternoon tea.

GINO'S TIP: Make sure the grapes are all dry before you add them so that they don't sink to the bottom of the cake.

Per serving	Kcal	Fat	Saturates	Carbs	Sugars	Fibre	Protein	Salt
	329	19g	6g	34g	23g	1g	3g	0.31g

INDEX

ACKNOWLEDGEMENTS

To everyone who worked on this book… I'm not going to do a list of names, but you know who you are.

First published in Great Britain in 2017 by Hodder & Stoughton

An Hachette UK company

3

A CIP catalogue record for this title is available from the British Library

Hardback ISBN 978 1 444 79522 6
Ebook ISBN 978 1 444 79523 3

Editorial Director: Nicky Ross
Project Editor: Lauren Whelan
Nutritionist: Kerry Torrens
Design & Art Direction: Alice Moore
Photographer: Tamin Jones
Food Stylist: Rosie Reynolds
Props Stylist: Jennifer Kay
Shoot Producer: Ruth Ferrier
Editorial Researcher: Helena Caldon
Copy Editor: Clare Sayer
Proofreader: Miren Lopategui
Indexer: Caroline Wilding

Typeset in Rockwell and Futura
Colour origination by Born
Printed and bound in Germany by Mohn Media

Hodder & Stoughton policy is to use papers that are natural, renewable and recyclable products and made from
wood grown in sustainable forests. The logging and manufacturing processes are expected to conform to the
environmental regulations of the country of origin.

Hodder & Stoughton Ltd
Carmelite House
50 Victoria Embankment
London EC4Y 0DZ

www.hodder.co.uk